TRADITIONAL INDIAN

CRAFTS

BY

MONTE SMITH

Eagle's View Publishing Company
6756 North Fork Road
Liberty, UT 84310

Library of Congress Catalog Card Number: 86-83379
ISBN 0-943604-13-3 in paperback

DEDICATION

To Michele VanSickle whose interest in, and knowledge of,
the culture and crafts of the American Indian
is an inspiration to all who know her and who
contributed greatly to this book.

12 11 10 9 8 7 6

TABLE OF CONTENTS

"Craft Techniques" Sections

INTRODUCTION

This volume was written in answer to numerous requests for a "how to do it" book that would not only cover the basics of the traditional craft of the American Indian, but would also present illustrated step-by-step instructions on how to do those crafts. There are a number of good books available that present hundreds of items of Indian craft but they fail to give good directions on how to go about constructing the items pictured and in many cases only those craftsman who know how to make them find the books of value.

This, however, is a book on the basics of Indian craft work, using readily available materials, that is written with two objectives in mind: First, it is directed to the person who simply wants to make a nice, attractive, yet authentic, choker or necklace (or whatever) and desires a clear, concise guide to producing that particular item. And, second, it will serve as a "primer" on the basics of traditional bone, leather and feather crafts of Native Americans for the craftsperson who wants to understand these techniques and thereby be able to construct items seen in the books mentioned above or in museums or described in historical sources.

How To Use This Book

In that many people will only want to construct two or three of the projects illustrated and explained in this text, the book is written so that you need only read the specific section that you are interested in. In other words, there is no need to read all of the section on feather work, in order to make a Single or Dancing Feather, or all of the bone section just to create a particular choker, etc. The drawback to this approach, of course, is that you will find a great deal of repetition if you read four or five of the projects at one time. For instance, almost every project includes a section that suggests that you read all of the instructions for that particular project before you start with *Step One* of construction and that you pre-plan your work. Be that as it may, each project was written independent of all others and the repetition should not be too bothersome and will, in any case, allow you to make any one item without reading the total book.

Along this line, and another reason why you should read the complete instructions before starting any project, is the inclusion of a "Hints" section that is at the end of the directions for almost every item covered herein. These are additional instructions and information that should make putting your craft item together much less difficult and will help you understand the process of creativity.

And, creativity is an important aspect that is, but should not be, overlooked in most basic books. For this reason there is a lot of stress on making changes in these projects at any stage where you feel it would help to make the item more suited to your particular taste and need. In all cases, not only the color and type of bead used is given but also the size so that you can "personalize" the item in any way you feel best. In other words, even though the "*Materials Needed*" list says to use an 8mm glass white heart bead, there is no reason why you could not use an 8mm plastic crow bead if your needs (aesthetic or financial) so direct.

Also included are a number of pages for "*Notes*." These may be found at the beginning and ending of each section and you are urged to use these to keep track of important aspects of your project and, especially, in any place where you change the construction from the given instructions. When, for example, you want to make another Feathered Dance Whistle just like the one you made from this book two years ago, your notes will be more than a little helpful. Further, when you find a technique that will help you put together a three feather brave's headdress, jot them down for later review. You will find it well worth the time and effort.

Other general information that can be applied to many of the projects in this book may be found in the "*Craft Technique*" segments. These are listed at the end of the "Table of Contents" and it may be helpful to consult the particular segment that is written about materials that are used in your specific craft item. For example, the segment on imitation sinew will be useful when constructing any item that calls for splitting this material, etc.

Materials

All of the materials used in these instructions are available from a number of sources. If you do not find them at your local craft store it is certain that they may be obtained at any store specializing in Indian and mountain man craft supplies. If you do not have such a store in your area, there are a number of very good "mail order" sources.

In all cases, the "*Materials Needed*" list should be considered the minimum material requirements. If, for instance, the project calls for 180 2-3" fluffs, the item will probably be more attractive if you use more. There are limits, of course, to this idea. In any event, never try to "get by" in using less materials than what is suggested.

Safety

As with any craftwork, there are certain hazards associated with doing Indian crafts. Using needles, awls, scissors, etc. can be dangerous if you are not careful and it is strongly suggested that you plan your work and do it with the necessary caution and care.

Acknowlegments

All of the graphics and photography for this book was done by R. L. (Smitty) Smith and his talent is self-evident. The text was read, proofed and re-proofed by Brad Schroeder who is therefore responsible for any and all errors that might remain (just kidding). Their assistance is greatly appreciated.

The greatest amount of credit for the production of this volume should go to Suzy whose unfailing love, support and encouragement continues to inspire and motivate.

TRADITIONAL INDIAN

CRAFTS

with

BONE

NOTES

BEAR CLAW

NECKLACE

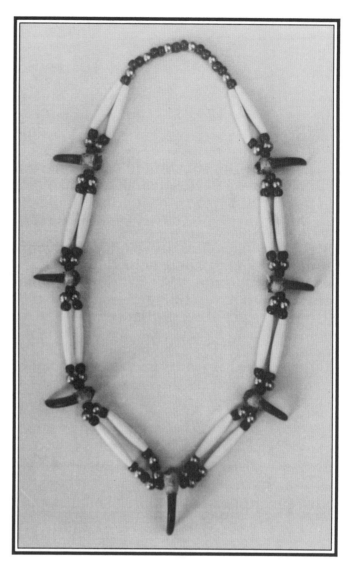

From the diaries of Hudson's Bay Company employees and the writings of LeClarc in the 1700s we have descriptions of *Claw Necklaces* made of bone, trade beads and clan symbols such as bear, cat and eagle claws. This kind of adornment can also be seen in the paintings of Catlin, Bodmer and others from the early 1800s, and it is possible to see examples in museums both in this country and in Europe that were collected from the American Indian by traders and sportsmen. The *Bear Claw Necklace* described below is a fairly simple, yet attractive rendition and could be made with almost any kind of large animal claw. The beginning hobbyist or scout might make this necklace using imitation bone hairpipe, hollow metal beads, pony beads and composition bear or eagle claws to produce a most appealing end product.

As with all craft projects, be sure that you understand all of the steps involved before you begin construction and do not be afraid to personalize the necklace to fit your own needs and taste.

MATERIALS NEEDED

16   1 1/2" bone hairpipe*
38   1/4" solid brass beads (large hole)
56   1/4" white heart beads^
7   Bear claws - drilled
6   Feet imitation sinew

(*) May be substituted with horn, antiqued bone or plastic hairpipe
(^) Any 1/4" bead of glass, bone, plastic or metal could be used

Figure 1

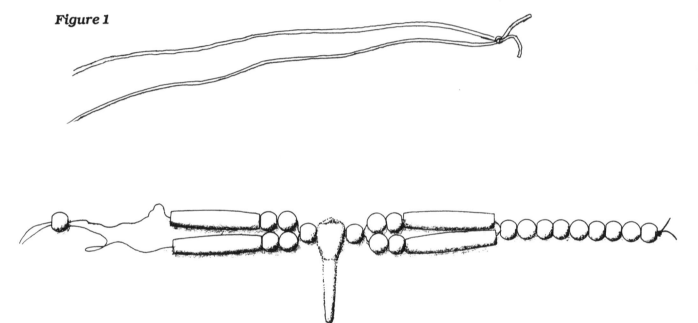

Figure 2

(1) For this project you will want to use the imitation sinew at full strength. Cut the suggested length into two pieces that are each 3' long. As shown in **Figure 1**, knot one of the ends of the two pieces together.

(2) Holding the other ends of both pieces of imitation sinew together, string 1 white heart bead, 1 metal bead, 2 white hearts, 1 metal bead, 2 white hearts, 1 metal bead and 1 white heart bead. Then (**Figure 2**), separate the two pieces of imitation sinew and string on each one: 1 hairpipe, 1 white heart and 1 metal bead. Now string both pieces through the same white heart and then both through one of the claws.

(3) String both pieces of imitation sinew through the same white heart, then separate the two pieces and string on each: 1 metal bead, 1 white heart, 1 hairpipe, 1 white heart, 1 metal bead and then string both pieces of the imitation sinew through the same white heart bead and then through a claw.

10

(4) Repeat *Step 3*.

(5) Thread both pieces of imitation sinew through the same white heart, then separate the two pieces and string on each: 1 metal bead, 1 white heart, 1 hairpipe, 1 white heart, 1 metal bead, 1 white heart, 1 metal bead and then take both pieces of imitation sinew through the same white heart, the middle (largest) claw and then another white heart. Separate the two pieces of sinew and string on each: 1 metal bead, 1 white heart, 1 metal bead, 1 white heart, 1 hairpipe, 1 white heart, 1 metal bead and then take both pieces through the same white heart and 1 claw (**Figure 3**).

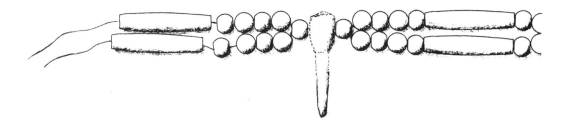

Figure 3

(6) Repeat *Step 3* two times.

(7) Bring the two pieces through the same white heart, then separate them and on each string place: 1 metal bead, 1 white heart, 1 hairpipe. Then bring the two pieces together again and string them through the same white heart, metal bead, 2 white hearts, 1 metal bead, 2 white hearts, 1 metal bead and 1 white heart.

(8) Be very careful as you tie off the finished necklace. If you make it too tight, it will crimp all of the material together; if it is too loose, the imitation sinew will show. Take your time. Undo the knot you made in Step 1 that tied the two ends of the two pieces together and tie the ends of each string together (**Figure 4**) with a neat, secure knot that may be hidden under the beads.

(9) After you are sure that the knot is secure and will not slip, remove the excess imitation sinew and hide the knots under one of the beads. Make sure that the imitation sinew is neither too tight nor too slack before doing this.

Figure 4

HINTS

(A) Genuine bone and horn hairpipe are hand made and often the pieces will be slightly different in size and shape. Therefore, before starting the project, place the hairpipe in pairs that are exactly the same and use these together in each segment of the necklace.

(B) Before beginning, arrange the claws in order of size. Use the two smallest at the top of the necklace (the first and the last one strung), working to the center (the fourth one strung) that should be the largest claw.

(C) If you have to purchase bear claws that are not drilled, it is fairly easy to drill a hole with a *Dremel© Tool* or a small drill bit. Be careful and make the hole just big enough for the two pieces of imitation sinew to pass through.

IMITATION BONE HAIRPIPE
BREASTPLATE

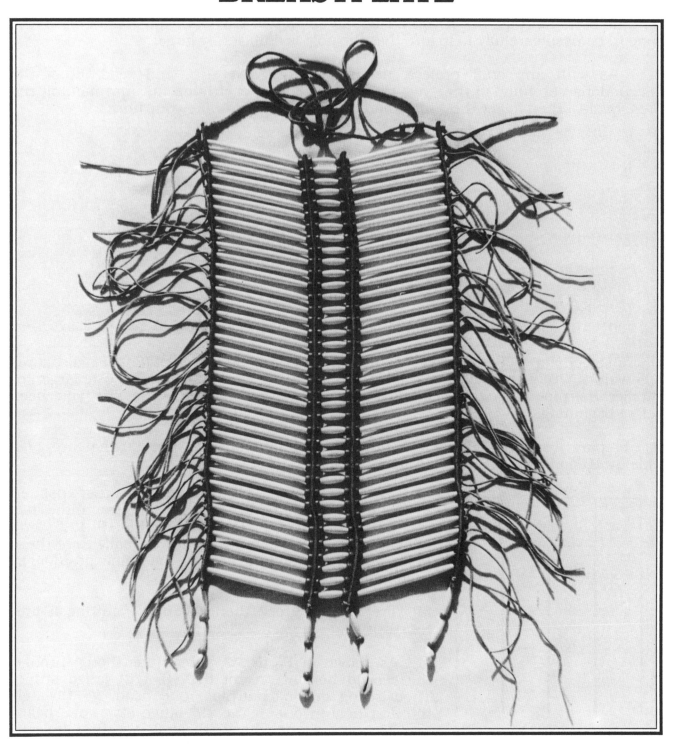

The *Hairpipe Breastplate* was worn by Indian warriors for protection of the vital chest area and today may be seen at pow wows and ceremonials. The style described below was designed by Joe Renville, a Sisseton Sioux, and is commonly seen at pow wows on the Plains. As described, it is made from imitation bone hairpipe as the goat thong requires a rather large hole. It could be made from genuine bone hairpipe but if you choose to do so you will want to examine all of the bone to be used carefully to insure that the hole is sufficiently large.

As with any craft project, before beginning be sure and read all of the instructions carefully so that you can visualize how each step fits into making the *Breastplate*. Then follow the instructions step-by-step and take your time.

MATERIALS NEEDED

1	Latigo piece 2 1/2" x 20"
2	Leather thongs - 30" each
4	Drilled cowry shells
50	Inches of imitation sinew
76	4" imitation bone hairpipe
47	1" imitation bone hairpipe
162	Glass crow beads*
76	Feet of greek thong

(*) Any glass or plastic bead about 9mm in size will work well.

The instructions will make an *Imitation Bone Hairpipe Breastplate* that measures 10" wide x 20" long. If you need a larger or smaller size, simply use larger or smaller hairpipe and longer latigo strips, etc. Make sure of the size you need before beginning.

(1) Prepare the latigo leather by cutting it into four strips: Two (2) that are 1/2" wide by 19" long and two (2) that are 1/2" wide by 19 1/2" long.

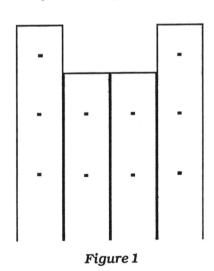

Figure 1

(2) With a leather punch, awl or other pointed instrument (Be Careful!), make 38 holes in the two 19" latigo strips and 39 holes in the 19 1/2" long latigo pieces. As shown in **Figure 1**, make sure these holes are evenly spaced and in the same position in each latigo strip.

(3) Prepare the greek thong lacing by cutting it into 38 strips that are each 24" long.

(4) As shown in **Figure 2**, thread one thong through the second hole of one of the 19 1/2" latigo strips. Then string one 4" hairpipe, one bead, go through the first hole in one of the 19" latigo strip, one bead, one 1" hairpipe, one bead, through the first hole in

the other 19" latigo strip, one bead, one 4" hairpipe and then through the second hole of the last 19 1/2" latigo strip. Now center the greek thong so that there is an equal amount showing on each side (about 6-7") and knot securely on the outside of the 19 1/2" latigo strips.

Figure 2

(5) Take another 24" piece of greek thong and string in the next hole down exactly as you did in Step 4. Continue this step until you have 37 rows completed; the bottom holes are left empty.

(6) Cut the imitation sinew into four (4) pieces that are 12" long. Take one piece and string it through one cowry shell until the shell is in the center of the sinew. Then take both ends of the sinew through 1 bead, one 1" hairpipe, 1 bead and one 1" hairpipe. Separate the sinew ends and tie through one of the bottom remaining holes, as shown in **Figure 3**, and knot securely. These knots will be exposed so make them secure and attractive. Repeat this step three times for the other bottom holes.

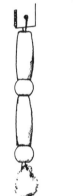

Figure 3

(7) Now use the two 30" leather thongs - these will hold the Breastplate in place, so make sure they are strong. Thread one of the thongs through the top hole of one of

Figure 4

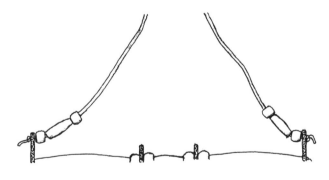

the 19 1/2" latigo strips leaving about 6" hanging on the outside and knot securely as you did with the greek thong on the rows below. Then, as shown in **Figure 4**, string one bead, one 1" hairpipe and 1 bead; then knot above the bead to keep this material in place. Repeat this step on the other 19 1/2" (or outside) strip. This will form the tie that goes around your neck.

(8) If you are going to use the *Breastplate* for dancing you will want to add a waist strap to hold it securely in place. Simply tie a leather thong to each outside latigo strip near the bottom so that it can be taken around your waist and tie in the back.

HINTS

(A) It is a good idea to lay out all of the materials as they will be used before starting. This makes it easier to locate what you need when you need it and will give you some idea of where you might want to make changes or use different color beads, etc. Do not be afraid to change the materials around or to personalize your *Breastplate*.

(B) If you choose to use genuine bone hairpipe be sure to check out all of the bone to be used to make sure that the hole through them is large enough and straight. 4" bone hairpipe is drilled 2" from one side and then 2" from the other and it is not uncommon for the hole to be slightly off from center; with greek thong, that will cause a problem. Also, bone hairpipe often differs slightly in size and you can improve the project a lot by taking account of these differences when laying the materials out before beginning construction.

HAIRPIPE BREASTPLATE

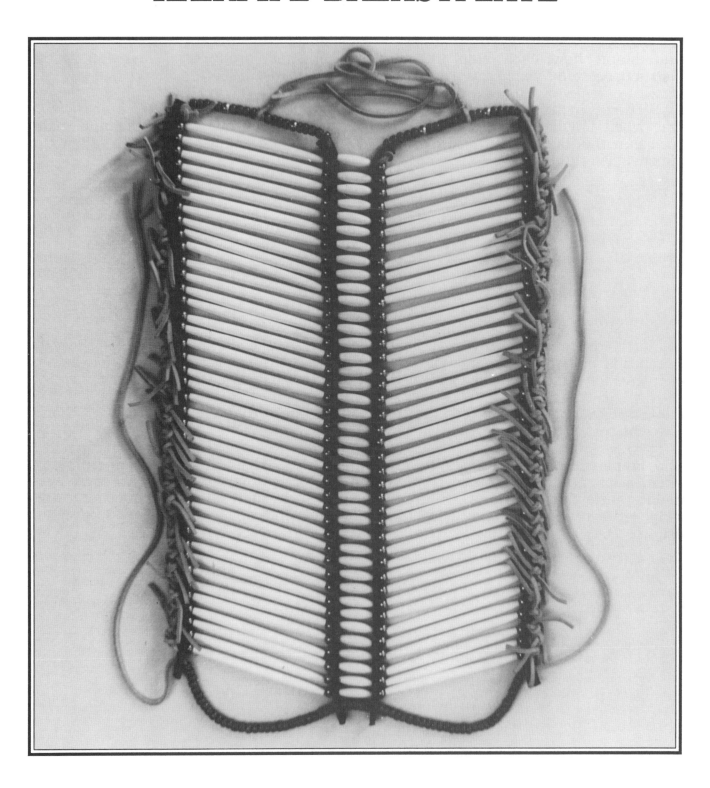

The *Hairpipe Breastplate* was worn by Indian warriors for protection against arrows and later, with the advent of the white man, the bone construction proved surprisingly effective at deflecting bullets! Today, Indians may be seen wearing *Breastplates* at pow wows and ceremonials.

Before beginning this project, read all of the instructions so that you understand how each step fits into the finished product. Then follow the instructions step-by-step, but be sure and take your time.

These instructions will make a *Breastplate* that measures 10" wide by 16" long when finished. The first thing to do is measure your chest area and make sure that this is the right size for you. If it has to be smaller or larger, adjust the dimensions and materials to fit you.

MATERIALS NEEDED

40	Feet suede leather thong
1	2" x 16" latigo strip
80	4" bone hairpipe
40	1" bone hairpipe
240	Glass trade beads*
15	Yards of imitation sinew

(*) You may use any large bead such as crow beads and it is a good idea to use beads of two colors and to arrange them in the project in a manner that is attractive to you. This makes a nicer Breastplate and personalizes it to your taste.

(1) Start by cutting 82 pieces that are 4" long each from the suede leather thong. Save the rest of the thong.

(2) Prepare the latigo leather by cutting 4 strips, each 1/2" wide and 16" long. Then, with an awl or other pointed instrument, punch 41 holes in each strip making sure that the holes are evenly spaced and exactly the same in each latigo strip. Start the first hole 1/4" from the end and space the holes 3/8" apart (**Figure 1**).

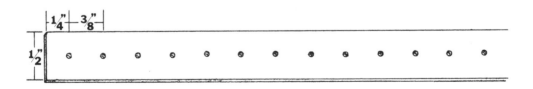

Figure 1

(3) As shown in **Figure 2**, tie the imitation sinew to the latigo strip just below the first hole, then take it through the hole so that it will be threaded down on the outside of the strip and go through the second hole. Tie one of the 4" suede leather thongs to the middle of this loop and then, on the sinew, string one bead, one 4" hairpipe, one bead, one latigo strip (again, through the second hole), one 1" hairpipe, one latigo strip (2nd hole), one bead, one 4" hairpipe, one bead and through the second hole of the last latigo strip.

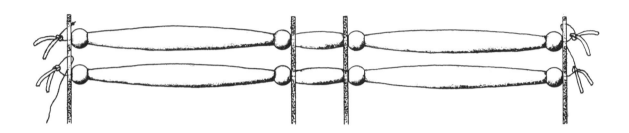

Figure 2

(4) Thread the sinew up through the outside of the top hole and back out of the second hole. Before you tighten this loop, tie on a 4" leather piece. Then tighten the whole row, leaving just a little slack.

(5) With the sinew coming out of the second hole, thread it down and into the third hole, tie on the leather 4" piece and string back as in *Step 3*. Continue until you have completed all 40 rows. Be sure that at the end of each row, including the last one, you take the sinew up through the next higher row and back through the same hole so that you can tie on the 4" suede leather thong. When completed, tie the sinew securely to the latigo strip.

(6) Cut two leather thongs that are 8" each. Tie one to the top right hole and string glass trade beads along the entire thong leaving enough of the thong to tie it to the right middle latigo strip. Tie the end through the top hole. Now repeat for the left side.

(7) Hold the Breastplate (in the middle of the thongs that were just put in place) up to your chest and position it where it should fit. Have someone measure the distance from the middle of the right thong (where you are holding it), around your neck to the middle of the left thong. Then cut two thongs to use to tie the Breastplate around your neck, leaving enough length for the knot. Tie these between the beads in the exact middle as shown in **Figure 3**.

(8) If you are going to use the Breastplate for dancing it is a good idea to add a waist strap. Measure from the outside of the Breastplate around your waist to the other side. Cut two thongs and tie one each to the outside latigo strip between the bottom two rows. Be sure and leave enough thong to make a tie.

(9) If you started with all of the materials listed above you should have some thong and beads left over and these may be used to decorate the bottom of the Breastplate.

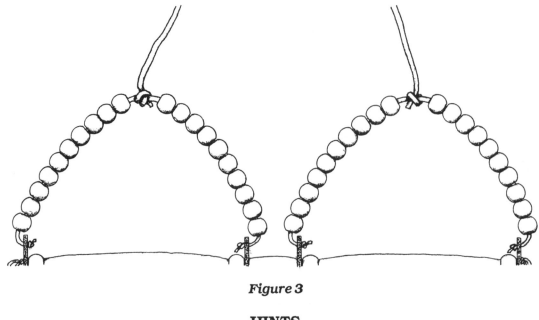

Figure 3

HINTS

It is suggested that you lay out the materials before beginning and decide how best to use the beads and hairpipe. As with all projects, it is also a good idea to look at books and visit museums for examples of old original pieces of this kind.

SIOUX DANCING CHOKER

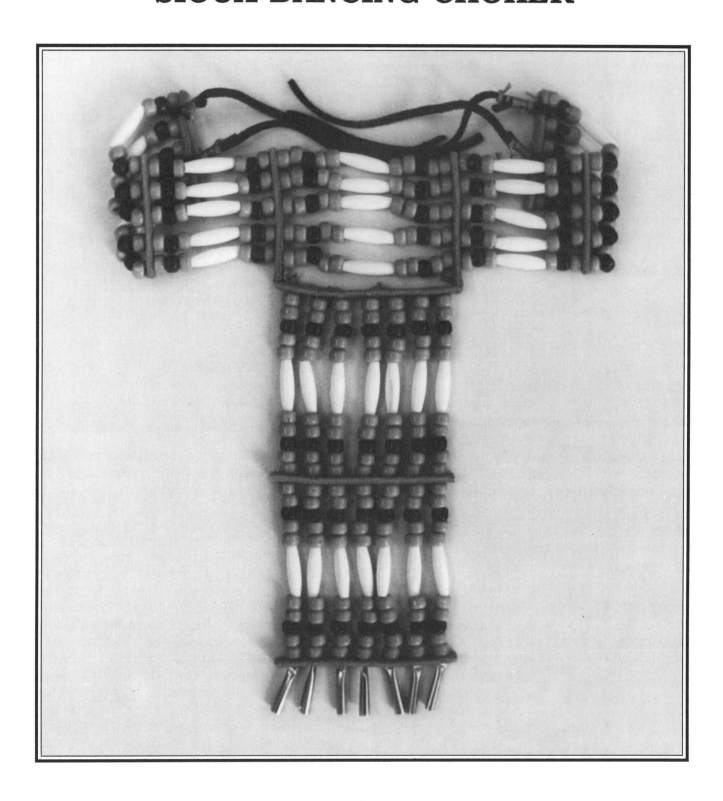

This is a classic choker that was, and is, seen among the Indians of the Plains. Actually a choker that is almost a necklace, this bone article is one of the few articles of adornment that were used by the woman of the family. And, while the bone chokers that were worn by the men of the Tribe were both functional, as they were used for protection during warfare, and decorative, this style choker was worn by the women as adornment only. Made of bone, the kinds of beads that were used depended upon the tribal influence. Today the fine choker may be seen at pow wows, ceremonials and rendezvous throughout the country.

As suggested in the "*Introduction*," it is a good idea to read all of the instructions thoroughly so that you understand how each step fits into making the finished product before you start putting it together. This will also allow you to decide if there is any place in the choker that you would like to "personalize" or change as it is made.

MATERIALS NEEDED

39	1" genuine bone hairpipe*
212	9mm glass crow beads ("A")^
98	9mm glass crow beads (corresponding color) ("B")^
1	Leather thong 24" long
13	Yards imitation sinew
7	Medium tin cones
7	Pony beads
1	Latigo leather piece 3 1/2" x 3 3/4"

(*) You may use antiqued bone, horn or plastic hairpipe
(^) Any 9mm bead of glass, bone, metal or plastic is suitable

(1) The first step is to make leather spacers from the latigo leather. For this project you will need four (4) spacers that are 2 1/4" long by 3/8" wide; two (2) spacers that are 2 1/2" long x 3/8" wide; and, three (3) leather spacers that are 3 5/8" long and 3/8" wide.

Figure 1

(2) Start with the leather spacers that measure 2 1/4" x 3/8": With one of these spacers, start at one end and measure in 3/16" and with a sharp pencil make a mark in the center (3/16" in from each side and 3/16" from the end). Then measure in from the other end the same distance and make another mark. Then exactly half-way between those two marks (this should be in the very middle of the spacers length) make a mark. Finally, between the middle mark and each outside mark, make another mark. You should now have five (5) pencil marks on the spacer and you want to put holes through the spacer at these points. **Figure 1** gives you an idea of what it should look like. The holes may be made with a small punch, awl or other sharp instrument but be careful as you do so. You are going to have to thread the artificial sinew through the holes, so make them big enough to get this material through them.

(3) Make holes in the other three (3) 2 1/4" x 3/8" spacers in exactly the same places as the one in *Step 2*.

(4) Next you want to make holes in the two (2) 2 1/2" by 3/8" leather spacers. It will help you visualize what this is suppose to look like if you have in mind what these two spacers are to be used for. Looking at the example of the finished choker shown, these are the two inner most vertical spacers in the project that are going to support the bottom, or hanging, part of the choker. To construct these, choose one end of one of the spacers (either end) that is going to be the top. Put one of the smaller spacers that was just finished (from *Step 2*) next to this one and punch holes exactly like you did above leaving excess at the bottom. Measure about 1/8" from the bottom end and place another hole at this point. Remember, this is going to support the weight of the bottom part of the choker so do not place this hole too close to the end (**Figure 2**).

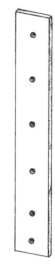

Figure 2

(5) Do exactly the same thing to the other 2 1/2" x 3/8" leather spacer.

(6) Place the spacers in front of you in this order: Two (2) short ones, two (2) longer ones (with the bottoms down) and the other two (2) short leather spacers.

(7) You will need about eighty (80") inches of imitation sinew to complete the first stringing sequence but, in that it will be easier to work with a shorter piece, feel free to cut off about 40" if you so desire. (Just make sure that if you choose to cut the imitation sinew, when it is necessary to add the extra length to complete the stringing that the knot is made in such a place as it will be hidden in the middle of one of the hairpipe or crow beads.) Further, the imitation sinew is about 500 pound test-strength nylon with bees wax impregnated into it so you may split it in half or thirds and still have enough strength to support the weight of the choker materials. This will also make stringing the leather spacers and beads much easier.

(8) Starting with the left-most spacer in front of you (if you are left handed, it will be easier to start with the right-most and the stringing sequence will be the same), run one end of the sinew you have cut through the top hole from the inside and tie it securely around the top hole. Now you are going to start stringing and to make it easier we will call the crow beads in the color that you have the most of ("A") and the color of crow beads that you have the least of ("B").

(9) On to the sinew, string: 1 A, 1 B, 1 A, 1 hairpipe, 1 A, 1 B, 1 A and then go

23

through the top hole of the next shorter spacer, then 1 A, 1 B, 1 A, 1 hairpipe, 1 A, 1 B, 1 A, then through the top most hole of one of the longer leather spacers, then 2 A, 1 B, 2 A, 1 hairpipe, 2 A, 1 B, 2 A then through the top most hole of the other longer leather spacer, 1 A, 1 B, 1 A, 1 hairpipe, 1 A, 1 B, 1 A, through the top hole of the third shorter spacer, 1 A, 1 B, 1 A, 1 hairpipe, 1 A, 1 B, 1 A and then through the top most hole of the last (end) shorter leather spacer. Pull snuggly, but not too tight and Do Not cut the imitation sinew.

(**10**) Hold the choker together (some help from another person will help here) and put it around your neck to make sure the size is right for you. If it is too short, just follow the rest of the instructions as the difference will be made up with the ties. However, if it is too long for you, it will be necessary to leave some of the materials out. The place to leave off material (either hairpipe or beads or both) is from each end. Just remember, if you leave something out on one side, you have to do exactly the same thing on the other side. If you leave out the first and last hairpipe you will lose about two (2") inches, if you leave off the entire side sections you will lose about five (5") inches and so forth.

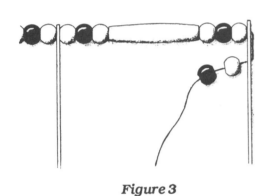

Figure 3

(**11**) When the choker is the proper length, take the sinew down (**Figure 3**) through the next hole and string in the exact sequence used above, in the top row, working your way back to the other end. Take the sinew down, from the outside, and through the next hole and continue this until you have five rows completed. Tie securely at the lower hole in the right-most end but make sure before tying that all of the rows hang evenly (that none of them droop down), but they should not be too tight either.

(**12**) The next step is to make the remaining leather spacers for the bottom portion of the choker. This is done exactly as you did above except that in this case you want three (3) leather spacers that measure 3 5/8" x 3/8" in length with seven (7) holes in each spacer so that you will have seven (7) vertical rows. After you have made the three exactly alike, choose one to be the top spacer and punch one (1) additional hole at each end. These holes will be used to attach the bottom portion of the choker to the two inside 2 1/2" vertical leather spacers at a later stage in the project. Place the three (3) drilled spacers horizontally in front of you with the top spacer at the top.

Figure 4

(**13**) Cut seven (7) pieces of imitation sinew that are

each ten (10") inches long. To the bottom of each piece of imitation sinew you want to attach a pony bead (or any small glass bead). To do this, string the imitation sinew through the hole in the bead, split the sinew into two pieces and tie these pieces together around the pony bead (**Figure 4**). Cut off the excess sinew around your knot.

(**14**) Now string a tin cone on each piece of imitation sinew so that the cone comes down to the end, comes over and hides the pony bead as seen in **Figure 5**. (This is an excellent technique that is used in many Indian craft projects and one that should be remembered).

Figure 5

(**15**) Choose one of the pieces of imitation sinew that has been prepared as described in *Step 13* and *Step 14* and thread it, from the bottom, through the bottom-most leather spacer at the right-most hole and string in the sequence: 2 A, 1 B, 2 A, 1 hairpipe, 2 A, 1 B, 2 A, and then through the right-most hole in the second (middle) leather spacer, then 2 A, 1 B, 2 A, 1 hairpipe, 2 A, 1 B, 2 A and finally through the right-most stringing hole (not the extra, outside hole made for tying) of the top-most horizontal leather spacer. Using the same technique used on the pony beads below, split the imitation sinew after you have gone through the hole, take the two ends around this leather spacer and tie neatly at the bottom so that your knot will be hidden by the top-most crow bead (**Figure 6**). You want this row to be held securely but not so tight that it causes the materials to "crunch" together; neither should it be so loose that you can see the imitation sinew between the beads.

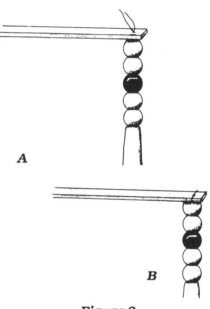

Figure 6

(**16**) Working to the left, repeat Step 15 until all seven (7) rows have been completed.

(**17**) The next step of the project is to attach the bottom portion of the choker to the top part. This step is very important to the way the choker will appear, so take your time and be careful. Run a piece of imitation sinew through the bottom hole of the right 2 1/2" spacer and another through the bottom hole in the left one. Take the imitation sinew attached to the right side through the right outside hole in the top 3 5/8" horizontal spacer and the imitation sinew attached to the left side through the left hole. Pull the bottom portion into place (**Figure 7**). You want this tie to be tight enough so that the bottom portion does not "droop" but

Figure 7

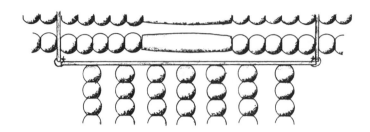

not so tight as to pull the center part together and out of position.   Before tying these pieces of sinew with knots, experiment so that it is just tight enough yet not too tight.

(18)   The final step is to attach neck thongs to the end spacers.   You may cut the thong into two (2) pieces and, in the exact center of each outside spacer, attach one thong using imitation sinew (**Figure 8**); or, you may cut the thong into four (4) pieces and attach a thong to each corner of the last spacer so that you will have a double neck tie.   In general, the double tie is less comfortable to wear around your neck but it does serve to keep the choker more even and attractive.

Figure 8

HINTS

(A)   The choker may be made from imitation bone hairpipe or from genuine bone or horn.   If you use genuine bone or horn you must keep in mind that these are products of "cottage industries" in the Orient and are made by hand.   As a result, they often vary slightly in size and shape and it is an excellent idea to lay out the project as it will be constructed so that you may match the bones and insure that those that are used in any one row are the same length.

(B)   If the project is pre-planned by laying it out as suggested above, you will be able to gauge the correct size of the finished choker and delete much of *Step 10*.   Be sure and keep notes as to what materials you have left out of each row, if any, for sizing requirements.

(C)   If you are interested in authenticity and are concerned with using the correct beads for a particular Tribe or Nation, it is recommended that you consult some good books on the subject and that you visit musuems that display original Indian artifacts if possible.

ERMINE TAIL CHOKER

The American Indian wore chokers to protect the vital neck area from injury by knife and arrow and with the intrusion of the white man, they proved surprisingly effective at deflecting ball and bullet. They were also a symbol of status with the inclusion of beads and animal furs. Today chokers may be seen at pow wows and ceremonials.

As with any craft project, be sure and read all of the instructions through carefully so that you understand how each step fits into the construction of the finished *Ermine Tail Choker* and so that you may choose any point where you want to change or personalize the project to fit your own needs or taste. Then follow the directions step-by-step and be sure and take your time as you do so.

MATERIALS NEEDED

24   Buffalo horn hairpipe (1 1/2")*
50   Glass faceted beads (8mm)^
 1   Light latigo (2 1/2" x 1 1/4")
 1   Suede thong (18")
 2   Ermine tails (medium or large)
 1   Abalone shell (1 1/2") drilled
 2   Tin cones (1")
 6   Feet imitation sinew

(*) May be substituted with imitation bone or genuine bone.
(^) May be substituted with 8mm plastic faceted, metal or bone beads.

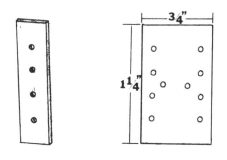

Figure 1   **Figure 2**

(1) Cut the latigo leather into five (5) pieces: Four (4) leather spacers that are 3/8" wide and 1 1/4" long and one (1) center piece that is 3/4" wide by 1 1/4" long.

(2) As shown in **Figure 1**, use an awl or other sharp, pointed instrument (Be Careful) and make four (4) evenly spaced holes in each of the spacers and two (2) additional holes in the middle of the center piece (these are for the shell and should match the holes in it) as shown in **Figure 2.**

(3) Push one end of the imitation sinew through the top hole of one of the spacers and tie it in place with a tight knot. Now string on the sinew: 1 bead, 1 hairpipe, 2 beads, 1 hairpipe, 1 bead, 1 leather spacer (go through an outside or "top" hole), 1 bead, 1 hairpipe, 1 bead, and then tie securely through the top hole of the center piece. _Do Not_ cut the imitation sinew.

(4) Thread the sinew down through the next outside hole of the center piece (**Figure 3**) and string 1 bead, 1 hairpipe, 1 bead, 1 leather spacer (through the next hole down), 1 bead, 1 hairpipe, 2 beads, 1 hairpipe, 1 bead, Tie securely to the outside spacer and go down through the next hole down. Repeat the stringing sequence in Step 3 and Step 4 when you tie tightly through the bottom hole of the outside spacer and cut the sinew. One side of the choker is now completed.

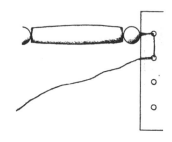

(5) Repeat *Steps 3 & 4* to complete the other side.

Figure 3

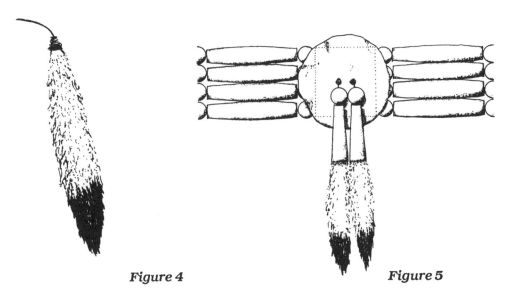

Figure 4   **Figure 5**

(6) As shown in *Figure 4*, secure one of the ermine tails to a 6" piece of imitation sinew. Then thread the sinew through one of the tin cones, slide the tin cone down over the ermine tail, and then string 1 bead. Repeat this to make up another piece. These dangles are then threaded through the holes in both the shell and the leather center piece (*Figure 5*) and tied together in the back. The knot should be secure but the dangles loose enough to allow them to hang down over the shell.

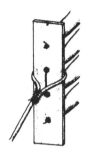

Figure 6

(7) Cut the leather thong to the desired size and tie one piece to each of the choker ends near the middle of the outside space (*Figure 6*). These thongs are used to tie the choker to your neck.

HINTS

(A) The materials list includes enough imitation sinew to use it full strength. However (depending upon the kinds of beads that you choose to use), it may be much easier to use the sinew if it is split into two or three strings. This will make it much easier to get the sinew through the beads and spacers, but it will still be strong enough to resist breaking.

(B) Should it be necessary to add imitation sinew while you are stringing, space the knot so that it will be hidden under one of the hairpipe. In that imitation sinew is waxed nylon, make sure that any knots are securely made!

(C) If you make the choker out of genuine bone or buffalo horn, keep in mind that these are hand made and often vary slightly in size and length. It is a good idea, therefore, to lay the choker parts out as they will be strung and match the hairpipe so that all of the rows will be exactly the same lengths.

(D) Also, laying the parts out will show you how long the choker will be when it is finished. It is designed for an "average" size neck and if you find it is too long simply take out some of the beads or hairpipe, if it is not long enough just add the needed material when you make it. This step will also help in finding out how long the neck thongs should be.

CRAFT TECHNIQUES

SIZING YOUR PROJECT

Most instructions are made for the "average" size person and may not be the exact size or shape that you need. As noted in most of the projects in this book, it is best to lay out all of the materials that will be used before starting construction as it will give you an idea of the dimensions of the finished item. If at this stage you find that the project will be too large or too small, you can plan ahead as to which materials should be added, to make it larger, or left out to make it smaller. You should make notes on this so that you will have them for reference later. Keep in mind, however, that most traditional Indian crafts have a "mirror" quality, or symmetry. That is, part of the beauty that is so appealing in Indian craft work is that there is a similarity of form or arrangement on either side of the project. What this means when you are sizing instructions to fit you is that what you do to one side of the center, should be done to the other side also. For example:

Project made from Instructions:

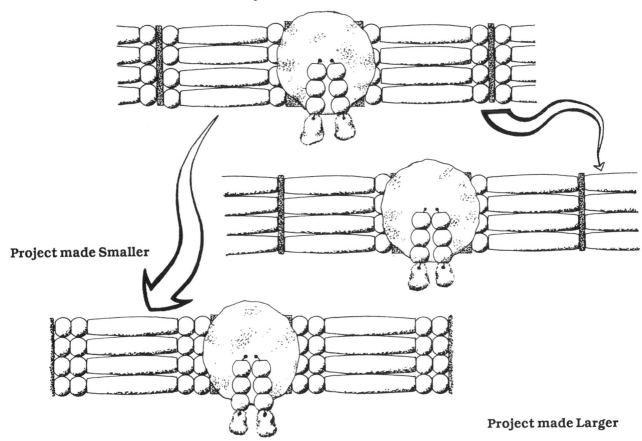

Project made Smaller

Project made Larger

WINNEBAGO TUBE & ABALONE CHOKER

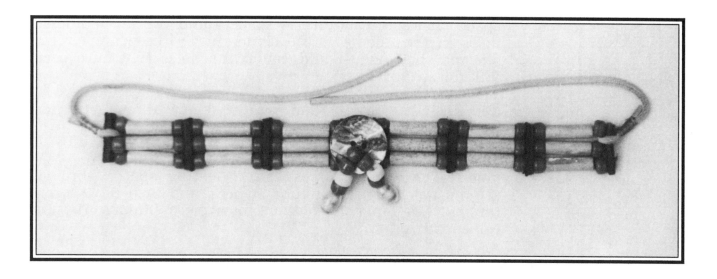

In order to protect the neck area of an Indian warrior while in battle, the choker was made from bone. It was also used to display wealth in the form of beads, claws, shell, etc. and to add to the overall fierce appearance of the man in warfare. The Indians, of course, had to make the hairpipe and tubes by working the bone into the proper shape and size and drilling the hole was truly a work of craftsmanship. Today, the choker is a standard part of the adornment of both men and women at pow wows and ceremonials.

Before starting to put your *Winnebago Tube and Abalone Choker* together, read the instructions through carefully so that you know how each step fits into making it. Do not be afraid to change or personalize your choker after you understand its construction.

MATERIALS NEEDED

18	Antiqued genuine bone tubes (1")*
43	Glass crow beads^
1	Latigo leather piece (4" x 1")
1	Abalone shell (1 1/2") drilled
2	Yards imitation sinew
1	Suede thong 20" long
2	Drilled cowry shells

(*) May be made with imitation bone, regular bone or horn tubes
(^) May be made from any 9mm glass, bone or metal bead.

(1) Cut the latigo leather into seven (7) pieces: Six (6) leather spacers that are 3/8" wide and 1" long and one (1) center piece that is 3/4" wide by 1" long.

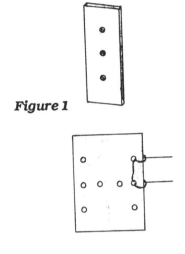

Figure 1

(2) As shown in **Figure 1**, use an awl or other sharp pointed instrument (Be Careful) and make three (3) evenly spaced holes in each of the spacers and two (2) additional holes in the middle of the center piece (these are for the abalone shell and should match the holes that have been drilled into it).

(3) Push one end of the imitation sinew through the top hole of one of the spacers and tie it in place with a tight, neat knot. Now string the sinew: 1 crow bead, 1 tube, 1 bead, 1 leather spacer (go through an outside or "top" hole), 1 bead, 1 tube, 1 bead, 1 leather spacer (through the top hole), 1 bead, 1 tube, 1 bead and then tie securely through the top hole of the center piece (**Figure 1**). Do Not cut the sinew.

(4) Thread the sinew down through the middle outside hole of the center piece and repeat the stringing sequence as outlined in *Step 3*. Be sure and go through the center hole in all of the leather spacers. Then tie to the middle hole on the outside spacer, go through the bottom hole and repeat the stringing sequence one more time. Tie tightly through the bottom hole of the center leather piece and cut the sinew. One side of your choker is now complete.

(5) Repeat *Steps 3* and *4* to complete the other side.

(6) As shown in **Figure 2**, string the imitation sinew through the center holes of the center piece and then through the holes in the shell. Now pass both ends of the sinew through 1 crow bead. Finish each end by stringing 3 beads, going through the hole in one of the cowry shells and knotting securely.

(7) Cut the leather thongs to the desired size and tie one piece to each end of the choker near the middle of the outside spacer (**Figure 3**). These thongs are used to tie the choker around your neck.

Figure 2

HINTS

(A) The materials list includes enough imitation sinew to use full strength. However, it will be much easier to use if it is split into two or three strings. This will make it easier to get the sinew through the beads and spacers but it will still be strong enough to support the choker and resist breaking.

(B)   Should it be necessary to add imitation sinew while you are stringing, space the knot so that it will be hidden under one of the tubes.

(C)   Genuine bone tubes (regular and antiqued) and buffalo horn are all made by hand and often vary slightly in length and size.   It is a good idea, therefore, to lay the choker parts out as they will be strung and match the tubes so that all of the rows are the same length.

Figure 3

(D)   Also, laying the parts out as they will be used will show how long the choker will be when it is finished.   It is designed for an "average" size neck, but if you find it is too long or too short, the inclusion or deduction of beads and/or tubes will allow you to make it just the right length.   This step will also help in finding out how long the neck thongs should be.

33

USING IMITATION SINEW

One of the most useful innovations to arts and crafts work has been the introduction of "imitation sinew." This product has an infinite number of threads made from nylon that have been wound together and impregnated with bees wax. It is great for almost any sewing or stringing project and, if used without splitting, has a test strength of about five hundred pounds. It is, however, a good idea to split the imitation sinew at times and the trick to doing this is to have someone hold the loose end as you pull the "strings" apart.

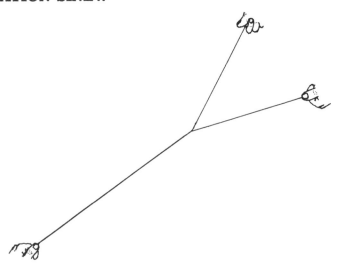

ANTIQUED BONE

Genuine bone hairpipe, tubes and beads are usually made from cattle bone from Brazil or the Orient and have an off-white color. As you can see from items in museums, as bone gets old it takes on a "mellow" brown color and the older it gets, the nicer it looks, so a lot of craftsmen prefer to use bone that has been made to look older with a technique called antiquing.

There are a number of ways to antique bone, but the easiest one is to fill an old pan with water, bring it to a slow boil and add four (4) teaspoons of tea. The best kind is an instant tea with lemon flavoring. Put the bone in the pan and stir continually for about five (5) minutes, checking the color occasionally. The longer it "cooks" the darker the color. Remove from water, spread bone out on absorbent paper and let dry.

TUBE STYLE CHOKER

Chokers were used by the American Indian both for protection while in battle and for adornment at dances and other ceremonial functions. This is a fairly simple *Tube Choker* but makes up into a most attractive finished product when complete.

As with all craft projects, it is a very good idea to read all of the instructions through carefully so that you understand how each step fits into making the completed *Tube Choker*. Then, follow along step-by-step and do not be afraid to change or personalize the instructions to make a product that fits your desires.

MATERIALS NEEDED

24   1" genuine bone tubes*
48   1/4" solid brass beads^
5   Feet of imitation sinew
1   20" leather suede thong
1   3" x 1 1/4" latigo piece

(*) You may substitute plastic, antiqued bone or horn tubes
(^) Any bead of metal, plastic, bone or shell may be used

(1) Cut the latigo leather into seven (7) leather spacers that are 3/8" wide by 1 1/14" long.

(2) As shown in *Figure 1*, use an awl or other sharp, pointed instrument (Be Careful) and make four (4) evenly spaced holes in each of the spacers.

(3) Push one end of the imitation sinew through the top hole of one of the spacers and tie it in place with a tight knot. Now string on the sinew: 1 bead, 1 tube, 1 bead, 1 leather spacer (go through an outside or "top" hole), 1 bead, 1 tube, 1 bead, 1 leather spacer, 1 bead, 1 tube, 1 bead, 1 spacer, 1 bead, 1 tube, 1 bead, 1 spacer, 1 bead, 1 tube, 1 bead and through the top hole of the last spacer. Do Not cut the imitation sinew.

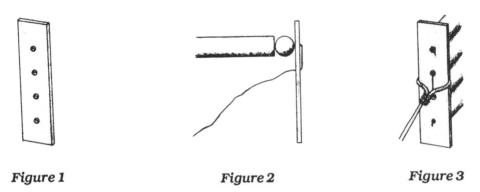

| Figure 1 | Figure 2 | Figure 3 |

(4) Thread the sinew through the next hole down (**Figure 2**) of the last spacer and repeat the stringing sequence in *Step 3.* When you have reached the last spacer on the other side, thread the sinew down to the next hole and do the stringing sequence once more. Then down through the last or bottom hole and finish stringing. Tie the sinew, with a neat knot, to the bottom hole on the outside spacer.

(5) Cut the leather thong to the desired size and tie one piece to each end of the choker near the middle of the outside spacer (**Figure 3**). These thongs are used to tie the choker to your neck.

HINTS

(A) The "materials" list includes enough imitation sinew to use it full strength. It will be easier, however, to use it if it is split into two or three strings. It will still be strong enough to support the materials in the choker and to resist breaking.

(B) Should it be necessary to add imitation sinew while you are stringing, space the knot so that it will be hidden under one of the tubes.

(C) If you are using genuine bone or horn, remember that these are made by hand and often vary in size and length. It is a good idea, therefore, to lay the choker parts out as they will be strung and match the tubes so that all of the rows will be the same length.

(D) Also, laying the parts out before beginning will show how long the choker will be when finished. It is designed for an "average" size neck, but if you find it too short or too long, simply leaving some of the materials out or adding some where needed will allow you to make it the correct size.

CLAW AND HAIRPIPE CHOKER

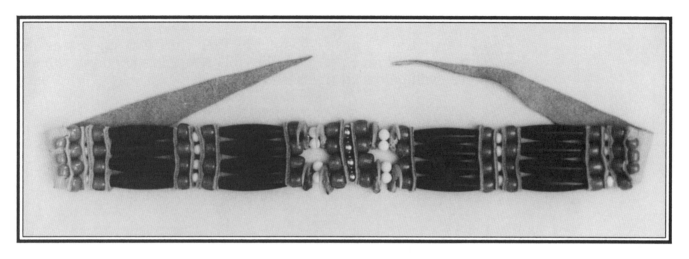

Chokers were used by the American Indian during warfare to protect the vital neck and throat area and as attractive adornment as part of their costume for "best dress" and ceremonials. Often coup or clan symbols were used as part of the choker and this *Claw and Hairpipe Choker* is an example of this.

This is a fairly difficult choker to construct and you should take special care to read all of the instructions through carefully before beginning so that you understand how each step fits into making the finished project. It is easy to personalize the *Claw and Hairpipe Choker* by changing the materials used or by positioning the beads in a different sequence; if you choose to do this, be sure that the choker retains the mirror effect (a balance of materials on each side).

MATERIALS NEEDED

16	1 1/2" horn hairpipe*
48	White heart beads - 1/4" or 8mm^
24	1/4" or 8mm round bone beads ^
6	White heart beads - 1/8" or 6mm^
4	1/4" solid brass beads^
1	Split leather piece - 6 3/4" x 1 1/4"
1	Split leather piece - 7" x 1 1/4"
8	Bobcat claws - drilled
6	Feet imitation sinew

(*) Could be genuine or plastic hairpipe or tubes
(^) Any of these beads could be substituted for glass, metal, bone or plastic beads of the same size as listed.

(1) Cut the 6 3/4" long split leather piece into eighteen (18) leather spacers that measure 3/8" wide x 1 1/4" in length as shown in *Figure 1*.

(2) Cut the 7" piece of split leather into two (2) pieces as shown in *Figure 2*. In the following instructions, these pieces will be called the ties.

Figure 1

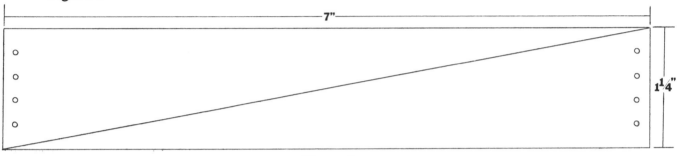

Figure 2

(3) As indicated on *Figures 1* and *2*, use an awl or other sharp, pointed instrument (Be Careful) and make four (4) evenly spaced holes in each of the spacers and about 1/8" from the large end on both of the ties. Be sure that these holes are exactly the same in all of the spacers and ties.

(4) Using a piece of imitation sinew (see "*Hints*" at the end of these instructions) that is about 6 feet long, tie securely to the outside or "top" hole of one of the split leather ties. Then start stringing (using the 1/4" beads of all materials) in this sequence: 1 white heart, 1 spacer (going through the top or outside hole), 1 bone bead, 1 spacer, 1 white heart, 1 spacer, 1 horn hairpipe, 1 spacer, 1 white heart, 1 spacer, 1 bone bead, 1 spacer, 1 white heart, 1 spacer, 1 hairpipe, 1 spacer, 1 white heart, through the top hole of one of the claws, 1 bone bead, another claw, 1 white heart, 1 spacer, 1 metal bead. This is the exact middle of the choker so now you continue stringing the sequence in reverse: 1 spacer, 1 white heart, through the top hole of one of the claws, 1 bone bead, the last claw, 1 red heart, 1 spacer, 1 hairpipe, 1 spacer, 1 white heart, 1 spacer, 1 bone bead, 1 spacer, 1 white heart, 1 spacer, 1 hairpipe, 1 spacer, 1 white heart, 1 spacer, 1 bone bead, 1 spacer, 1 white heart and then through the outside or "top" hole in the other split leather tie. This completes the first row of your choker but Do Not cut the imitation sinew.

(5) Thread one of the small white heart beads on the sinew and then take it back through the split leather tie at the next hole (the 2nd) down. In this row, use the same material as was used in the first or top row except that you go through the bottom holes in the claws and then continue as above until you reach the split leather tie at the other end.

(6) As shown in *Figure 3*, when the second row is complete string one small white heart on the sinew and take it back through the first hole (above), through the first white heart, down and back out of the second white heart and the second hole. Then place another small white heart on the sinew and go back through the leather tie at the next hole (third) down.

(7) The third row is essentially strung in the same sequence as was done in *Step 4* with the incorporation of four (4) more claws by going through the top hole in all of them. However, when you reach the end of this row you want to add a small white heart on the outside of the leather tie between the second and third rows and the third and fourth rows just as you did in *Step 6*.

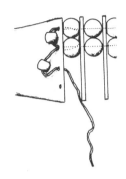

Figure 3

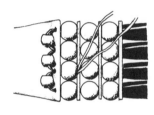

Figure 4

(8) When you have the small white heart in place, use the stringing sequence as you did in *Step 5* until you reach the split leather tie, then incorporate the small white heart as was done in *Step 6* by going back up through the third hole, through the first white heart of that row, split the imitation sinew into two parts (*Figure 4*) and make a small, neat knot that will be hidden between that white heart and the leather spacer. This will effectively hide your knot and still be very secure if the knot is tight.

HINTS

(A) The amount of imitation sinew noted in the *"Materials Needed"* list is sufficient so that it may be used full strength. However, it will be much easier to use if it is split into two or three strings. This will make it easier to get the sinew through the beads and spacer holes but it will still be strong enough to resist breaking and to support the materials on the choker.

(B) In that this project uses split leather instead of latigo leather for the spacers, it may be much easier to string everything if you use a Glover's or leather needle. If you choose to do this, it will be almost a necessity to split the sinew into three or four strings, but that will still be very strong and much easier to thread the needle.

(C) Should it be necessary to add imitation sinew while you are stringing, space the knot so that it will be hidden under one of the hairpipe. It may be that you will want to use smaller lengths of imitation sinew than suggested in the instructions, as it will be easier to string, and add other lengths as instructed here as you progress with the choker.

(D) If you have to drill the claws you may use a *Dremel©* tool or a very small drill bit. Be very careful as the holes are drilled and pre-plan how the claws will be

TOP ROW
CLAW

BOTTOM ROW
CLAW

Figure 5

used. As four (4) of the claws will be used on the top two rows, the holes for these should be drilled lower than those hole in the other four, or bottom, claws (see **Figure 5**). In any event, the holes in the claws should be exactly the same distance apart as the holes in the spacers and ties.

(E) Any time you use genuine bone or horn tubes and hairpipe, remember that these are made by hand and, therefore, may vary slightly in size and shape. It is a good idea to lay the choker parts out as they will be strung before constructing the project and match the hairpipe so that all of the rows will be the same length.

(F) Also, laying out the parts before starting to string will show how long the choker will be when it is finished. The instructions herein will make a choker that will fit the "average" adult size neck, but if you find that it is too long or too short, simply add or delete some of the materials so that it will fit just right.

(G) By laying out all of the materials before beginning, it will also allow you to plot the exact length of the split leather ties.

SINGLE CLAW AND TUBE CHOKER

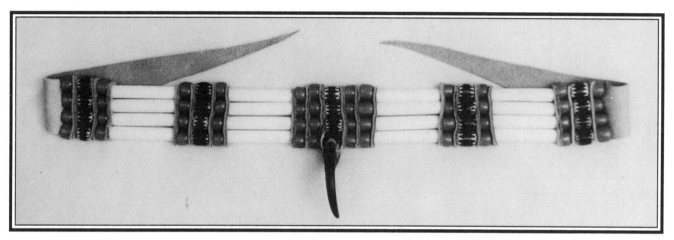

Bone chokers were worn by Indian warriors to protect the vital neck and throat area from injury by knife and arrow. Later, with the coming of the white man, they proved effective even against ball and bullet. They were also an intricate part of "best dress" for dancing and other ceremonial events and as such, often displayed beads, claws and furs as symbols to status, wealth and/or clan. Today chokers are seen at pow wows, ceremonials and rendezvous throughout the country.

The *Single Claw and Tube Choker* is a fairly easy choker to construct but the inclusion of a claw makes a very attractive addition and, while this rendition includes a bear claw, almost any kind of claw or tooth could be attached. It is important to first read all of the instructions included through carefully so that you understand how each step fits in toward completing the finish product. If you want to change any of the steps in order to personalize the choker, plan those as you read and then, while incorporating your own ideas, take your time and work toward a finished choker.

MATERIALS NEEDED

16	1 1/2" bone tubes*
48	8mm or 1/4" white heart beads^
20	8mm or 1/4" chevron beads^
1	Split leather piece - 7" x 1 1/4"
1	Split leather piece - 7 1/2" x 1 1/4"
6	Feet imitation sinew
1	Drilled bear claw - large

(*) May be substituted for with antiqued bone, horn or plastic
(^) Any bead of plastic, glass, bone or metal may be used

(1) Cut the 7 1/2 long split leather piece into twenty (20) leather spacers that measure 3/8" wide x 1 1/4" long (*Figure 1*).

Figure 1

(2) Cut the 7" split leather piece into two (2) pieces as shown in **Figure 2**. These will be the leather ties for your choker.

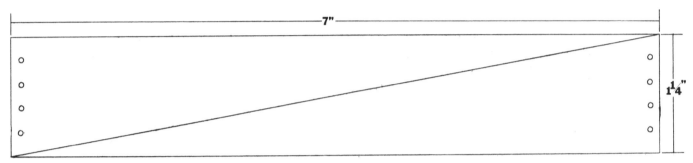

Figure 2

(3) As noted on both **Figure 1** and **Figure 2**, use an awl or other sharp, pointed instrument (Be Careful) and make four (4) evenly spaced holes in each of the spacers and about 1/8" from the large end on both of the·ties. Make certain that these holes are exactly in the same position in all of the spacers and ties. NOTE: In that this project uses split leather instead of latigo leather for the spacers and ties, it may be easier to string everything if you use a Glover's or leather needle. If you choose to do this, it will be a near necessity to split the sinew into three or four strings. This will still be strong enough to support all of the materials in the project,

(4) Using a piece of imitation sinew that is about 5 feet long, tie it securely to the outside or "top" hole of one of the split leather ties. Then start stringing in this sequence: 1 white heart, 1 spacer, 1 chevron bead, 1 spacer, 1 white heart, 1 spacer, 1 tube, 1 spacer, 1 white heart, 1 spacer, 1 chevron bead, 1 spacer, 1 white heart, 1 spacer, 1 tube, 1 spacer, 1 white heart, 1 spacer, 1 white heart, 1 spacer, 1 chevron bead (this is the center bead), 1 spacer, 1 white heart, 1 spacer, 1 white heart, 1 spacer, 1 tube, 1 spacer, 1 white heart, 1 spacer, 1 chevron bead, 1 spacer, 1 white heart, 1 spacer, 1 tube, 1 spacer, 1 white heart, 1 spacer, 1 chevron bead, 1 spacer, 1 white heart and then through the outside or "top" hole of the other split leather tie. Do Not cut the imitation sinew.

(5) Now take the imitation sinew down and through the hole just beneath the top one (the second row) in the split leather tie. Then start stringing in this sequence: 1 white heart, 1 spacer, 1 chevron bead, 1 spacer, 1 white heart, 1 spacer, 1 tube, 1 spacer, 1 white heart, 1 spacer, 1 chevron bead, 1 spacer, 1 white heart, 1 spacer, 1 tube, 1 spacer, 1 white heart, 1 spacer, 1 white heart, 1 spacer, 1 chevron bead (this is the center bead), 1 spacer, 1 white heart, 1 spacer, 1 white heart, 1 spacer, 1 tube, 1 spacer, 1 white heart, 1 spacer, 1 chevron bead, 1 spacer, 1 white heart, 1 spacer, 1 tube, 1 spacer, 1 white heart, 1 spacer, 1 chevron bead, 1 spacer, 1 white heart and then through the second hole of the first split leather tie.

(6) Take the imitation sinew down through the next hole (3rd) down, go through the tie and repeat the stringing sequence in *Step 4*.

(7) Then down through the final hole in the tie and follow the stringing as given in *Step 5*. When you reach the last split leather tie, make a good, secure, neat knot on the outside - this knot will be hidden by the tie when the choker is worn.

(8) String the drilled bear claw on to a 6" piece of full strength imitation sinew. Take one end of the sinew through the hole in the middle (center) chevron bead in the third (second from the bottom) row (*Figure 3*) and tie a small, neat knot at the extreme edge of this bead to hold the claw in place. The idea is to have the claw secure but with enough sinew so that it will rest against your throat. Further, you want the base of the claw and not the end (sharp point) to rest against your body!

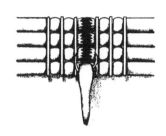

Figure 3

HINTS

(A) With the amount of imitation sinew listed in the "Materials" above, there will be enough to use it full strength for all stringing. It will, however, be much easier to use if it is split into two or three strings. This will, of course, make it easier to get the imitation sinew through the beads, spacer and tie holes and it will still be strong enough to resist breaking. If you are uncertain about the strength, or just want to tidy up the appearance of the finished choker, you may want to take the sinew through all of the stringing sequence twice. This does make the choker tighter, so do not string without some amount of "give."

(B) Should it be necessary to add imitation sinew while you are stringing, be sure and plan the knot so that it will be hidden under one of the tubes. It may be that you will want to use smaller lengths of imitation sinew than suggested, as it will be easier to string with less "thread." Adding other lengths is easy if you plan ahead so that the knots are hidden inside the bone tubes.

(C) If you have to drill the claw (or teeth or whatever you choose), the best tool to use is a Dremel© instrument or a very small drill bit. Be careful when you drill the hole and make it just big enough to pass the imitation sinew (full strength) and not large enough to let the claw dangle loose (*Figure 4*).

Figure 4

(D)   Genuine bone and horn tubes are all made by hand and any time you use these materials you must note that they will often vary in size and shape.   Therefore, it is a good idea to lay the choker parts out in front of you before construction as they will be strung so that you can match all of the bone or horn tubes in rows of equal length.

(E)   Further, laying out the parts before you string them together will show you how long the choker will be when finished.   Most instructions are for chokers that will fit an "average" adult neck and you may find that it is too long or too short for you.   If this is the case, by pre-planning you can add or leave off materials so that the choker will fit exactly as you desire.

(F)   Another way to adjust the length of the choker is by shortening or lengthening the split leather ties.   If you have pre-planned your construction by laying out the project before putting it together, you can easily gauge the proper length of these ties.

MOUNTAIN MAN CHOKER

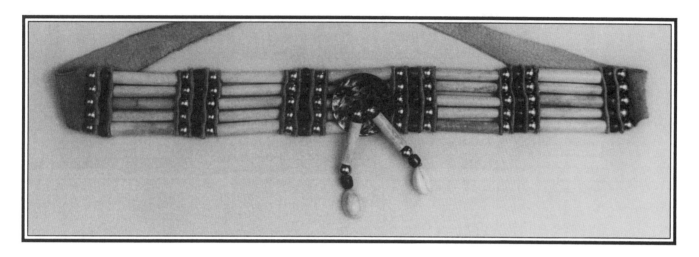

The American Indian used a bone choker to protect his neck from enemy arrows and later from ball and shell. He would also exhibit his status and wealth by incorporating beads, claws, cones, etc. into the making of the choker. With the advent of the fur traders and mountain men, they soon adopted Indian-style clothing and adornment and the *Mountain Man Choker* is a sample of some of the innovations that were possible with the availability of trade and metal beads. Today, chokers may be seen at pow wows, ceremonials and rendezvous.

Read the instructions through carefully before you begin constructing your *Mountain Man Choker* so that you know how each step fits into making the finished project. Do Not be afraid to change or personalize the choker so that it fits your personal needs. Then, follow the instructions.

MATERIALS NEEDED

1	8" x 1 1/2" split leather piece
1	7" x 1 1/2" split leather piece
27	1 1/2" antigued bone tubes*
32	8mm white hearts^
54	1/4" hollow brass beads#
7	Feet imitation sinew
1	1 1/2" abalone shell - drilled
2	Cowry shells - drilled

(*) You may use imitation bone, regular bone or horn tubes
(^) 8mm beads of plastic, glass, bone or metal may be used
(#) Complimentary beads of plastic, glass or bone may be used

Figure 1

(1) Cut the 8" x 1 1/2" split leather piece into twenty (20) leather spacers that are 3/8" by 1 1/2" long (**Figure 1**).

(2) Cut the 7" x 1 1/2" split leather piece into two (2) pieces as show in **Figure 2**.

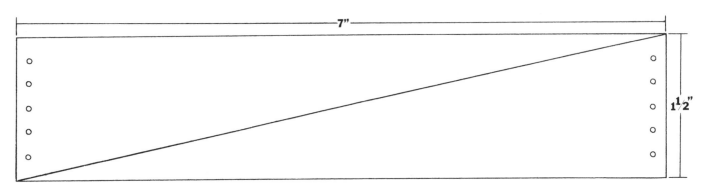

Figure 2

(3) As shown in **Figure 1** and **2**, use an awl or other sharp, pointed instrument (Be Careful) and make five (5) evenly spaced holes in each of the spacers and about 1/8" from the large end on both of the split leather (*Step 2*) pieces.

(4) (For the stringing sequence below, "MB" means Metal Bead and "Bead" means White Heart Bead.) Using a piece of the imitation sinew (see "Hints" at the end of these instructions) that is about 6 feet long, tie securely to the outside or "top" hole of one of the split leather pieces from *Step 2*. Then start stringing in this order: 1 MB, 1 leather spacer (going through an outside or "top" hole), 1 bead, 1 spacer, 1 tube, 1 spacer, 1 MB, 1 spacer, 1 bead, 1 spacer, 1 MB, 1 spacer, 1 tube, 1 spacer, 1 MB, 1 spacer, 1 bead, 1 spacer, 1 MB, 1 spacer, 1 tube, 1 spacer, 1 MB, 1 spacer, 1 bead, 1 spacer, 1 MB, 1 spacer, 1 tube, 1 spacer, 1 MB, 1 spacer, 1 bead, 1 spacer, 1 MB, 1 spacer, 1 tube, 1 spacer, 1 bead, 1 spacer, 1 MB and then through the top hole of the other split leather piece from *Step 2*. Do Not cut the imitation sinew.

(5) Thread the sinew through the next hole down (**Figure 3**) on the split leather piece and repeat the stringing sequence in *Step 4*. When you have reached the split leather piece on the other side, thread the sinew down to the next hole and do the stringing sequence once more. Repeat this sequence twice more until you reach the fifth, or "bottom" row. Tie the sinew, with a neat knot, around this leather piece and cut off the excess imitation sinew.

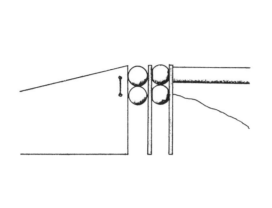 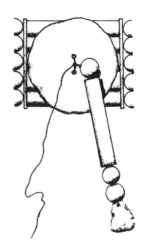

Figure 3	*Figure 4*

(6) Wrap the middle of a 12" piece of imitation sinew around the middle of the center tube in the middle row and thread each end through one of the holes in the abalone shell and knot securely. On one end of the imitation sinew string 1 MB, 1 tube, 1 MB, 1 bead and then go through the hole in one of the cowry shells and tie securely. Cut off the excess imitation sinew. Repeat this step on the other end of the imitation sinew as shown in *Figure 4*.

HINTS

(A) The amount of imitation sinew noted in the "Materials Needed" list is sufficient so that it may be used full strength. However, it will be much easier to use if it is split into two or three "strings." This will make it easier to get the sinew through the beads and spacer holes but it will still be strong enough to resist breaking and to support the materials on the choker.

(B) Should it be necessary to add imitation sinew while you are stringing, space the knot so that it will be hidden under one of the tubes.

(C) Any time you use genuine bone (antiqued or regular) or horn tubes or hairpipe, remember that these are made by hand and, therefore, may vary slightly in size and shape. It is a good idea to lay the choker parts out as they will be strung and match the tubes so that all of the rows will be the same length.

(D) Also, laying the parts out before starting the project will show how long the choker will be when it is finished. These instructions will make a choker that will fit the "average" neck, but if you find that it is too long or too short, simply add or delete some of the materials so that it will fit just right.

(E) By pre-planning or laying out all of the materials before beginning, it will also allow you to plot the length of the ties (leather piece from *Step 2*).

NOTES

TRADITIONAL INDIAN

CRAFTS

with

LEATHER

NOTES

SMALL LEATHER

POUCH

In the daily life of the American Indian, pouches and bags played a very important part. There were, of course, no pockets or handbags in which to carry things and almost anything of value or utility had to be carried in a pouch. The *Small Leather Pouch* featured in these instructions is a typical pouch construction and with these techniques you can make a container of almost any size. If you are interested in other pouches, bags and containers, please see *Traditional Indian Bags, Pouches and Containers* by Monte Smith.

MATERIAL NEEDED

1   Split leather piece 6" x 5"
1   Suede thong 12" in length
1   Yard imitation sinew
1   #8 Glover's or leather needle

(1) Cut the leather following the pattern (*on next page*) in these instructions. Then fold it lengthwise, so that you have a pouch 3" x 5.

(2) Split the imitation sinew into three or four pieces and thread one of the pieces on the Glover's needle. Using a whip stitch (**Figure 1**), sew the bottom and side together.

(3) Turn the bag inside out so that the sewing is hidden inside and 1/2" from the top of the bag punch 6 holes as shown on the pattern.

(4) Thread the 12" suede thong through the holes and knot the ends.

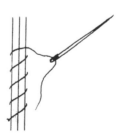

Whip Stitch

51

HINTS

(A) Take your time as you put the project together. Think about how everything goes together and if you want to make any changes, plot how to make them part of the finished project.

(B) The imitation sinew may be used full strength, but it will be easier to use on the needle, and still be very strong, if it is split into three or four "threads."

(C) Be sure and hide all of the knots in the imitation sinew so that they will be hidden inside of the leather pouch.

(D) If the leather is to be beaded it will be much easier to do so before the pouch is sewn together. For ideas on decoration and adornment it is a good idea to visit museums or consult books such as *The Techniques of Porcupine Quill Decoration Among the Indians of North America* by Wm. Orchard, *The Techniques of North American Indian Beading* by Monte Smith, *Crow Indian Beadwork* by Wildschut and Ewers and *Beads and Beadwork of the American Indian* by Wm. Orchard.

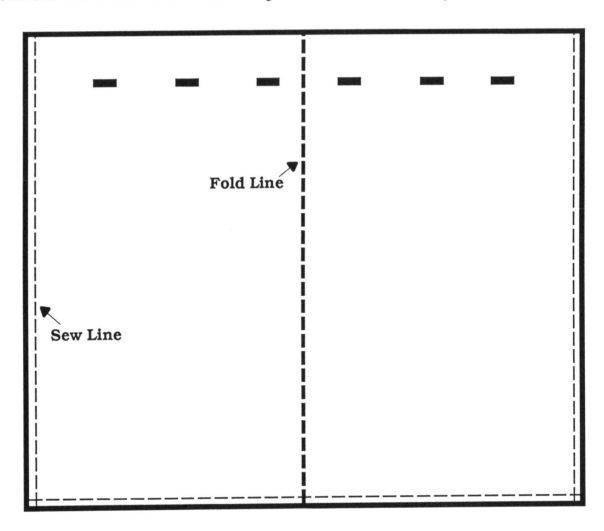

MEDICINE POUCH

NECKLACE

In almost every Indian Nation it was common for the People to have a special pouch that they carried with them at all times in which to carry their personal medicine. These pouches took many shapes and forms and this one, designed after one that may be seen in the museum at Cody, Wyoming from the Nez Perce, is but one variation. It was selected for inclusion here as many of the techniques may be used in many different craft projects and because it is a most attractive addition to any traditional costume when finished.

As with any craft project, we suggest that you first read through all of the instructions so that you know how each step fits into making your *Medicine Pouch Necklace*. When you have these in mind, follow the instructions through step-by-step but take your time so that the pouch will be made the best way possible. Do not be afraid to change or personalize the project in any way that is appealing to you and remember that, as with most leather projects, if you are going to decorate the pouch with paint, beads or quills you should do so before sewing it together.

The instructions include both a variation for using imitation bone hairpipe and one for genuine bone hairpipe. The technique described for genuine bone hairpipe is more challenging and may be used with the imitation bone.

MATERIALS NEEDED

1	2" circle of split leather
1	24" suede thong
1	Yard imitation sinew
1	#8 Glover's needle
2	1" imitation bone hairpipe, or
2	1" genuine bone hairpipe
30	Glass crow beads

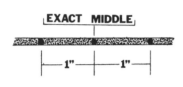

Figure 1

(1) First, measure the thong around your neck leaving room to tie it in the back. Remember, the pouch is not a choker but a necklace that should rest about 2" below your "adam's apple." Cut off the excess thong if there is any. Find the exact middle of the thong and make a mark with a pencil, then measure 1" from both sides of the center mark and make two more pencil marks. You should now have a 2" space marked out in the middle of the thong.

(2) Following the pattern to the side, cut a circle from your split leather that is exactly 2" in diameter and perfectly round. Then follow either the instructions in *Step 3a* or *Step 3b* as you prefer.

(3a) This is how most traditional pouches of this kind were made: Place the leather circle in the exact middle of the thong, so that it matches the marks made in *Step 1*. Fold the leather over the thong and, starting at one side, use the imitation sinew and leather needle, and with a whip stitch, sew around the half circle to the middle. If you want to put your personal "keep safe" or "medicine" inside the pouch, place it inside at this point. Then continue sewing around the pouch until it is completely closed. Keep in mind that with this method the stitches and knots will be exposed, so make nice evenly spaced stitches and good tight, small knots. Then go to *Step 4*.

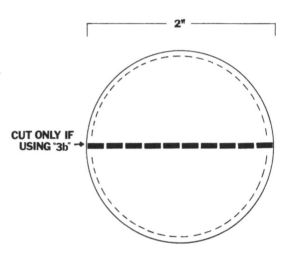

Figure 2

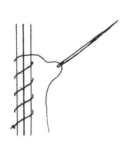

Whip Stitch

(3b) This more contemporary method allows you to hide most of the stitches and knots: Cut the leather circle into two half circles. Then, using the whip stitch, sew the round sides of the pouch together starting 1/8" from the top of one side and ending 1/8" from the top of the other side. Do not sew the top (where you cut the circle in half) together. Turn the bag inside out so that the sewing is hidden inside. If you want to put your personal "keep safe" or "medicine" inside the pouch, place it inside at this time. Place the pouch in the center of the thong (matching the marks made above in *Step 1*) so that the 1/8" space that was not sewn comes around the thong. Then sew the top of the two sides together making an evenly spaced whip stitch. With this method only the stitch that is hidden by the thong and the final knot needs to show. Make a good tight, small knot.

(4) From one end of the thong, string 1 crow bead, 1 imitation bone hairpipe and then 14 more crow beads so that they are next to the pouch. Then from the other side of the thong, repeat the stringing as you did on the other side.

(5) Tie the necklace around your neck. A square knot works well with leather thongs.

Variation with Genuine Bone Hairpipe

(6) It may be difficult, if not impossible to string real bone hairpipe on to a leather thong. The way to progress, if you find this is the case, is to mount the Medicine Pouch to the center of an 8" piece of full strength imitation sinew. Then add one crow bead to each side and then the bone hairpipe.

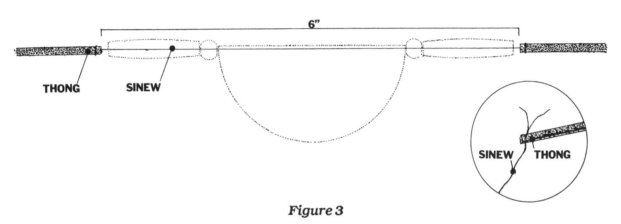

Figure 3

(7) Now cut the thong into two pieces. At about 1/8" from the end of one thong use the needle and make a hole. Then, with the needle, push one end of the 8" piece of imitation sinew (with the pouch, beads and hairpipe already on it) through the hole and pull about 1" of the sinew through. Split the sinew, take each half around opposite sides of the thong and make a small knot. Trim off any excess. Do the same thing on the other side (see *Figure 3*). Then do the stringing sequence as described above. When you finish, the beads will cover where the thong and the imitation sinew are joined and some of the thong will have to be trimmed to make a good fit around your neck.

HINTS

(A) If you follow the list of *Materials Needed* there is plenty of imitation sinew to allow you to sew with it as it is. However, it will be easier to sew with, and much easier to thread the needle, if the sinew is split into three or four "threads." It will still be strong enough to be sturdy in sewing and will not break. For stringing, however, the imitation sinew should be used full strength.

(B) Any decoration with paints, quills or beads will be easier to do before sewing the pouch together. Be sure, however, to leave about 1/8" from the side for sewing.

(C) If you find that it looks like there are too many crow beads on the thong when you wear the necklace pouch, simply leave some of them off of it. Also, do not be afraid to rearrange the tubes and crow beads or to use crow beads of two different colors to match your personal preference.

(D) If you are going to custom decorate your Medicine Pouch Necklace, two good books on the subject are **The Techniques of Porcupine Quill Decoration Among the Indians of North America** by Wm. C. Orchard and **The Techniques of North American Indian Beading** by Monte Smith. Both books give complete instructions on how to decorate with traditional techniques. Also, looking at good books or going to a museum is great for getting decoration ideas.

QUILLED MEDICINE WHEELS

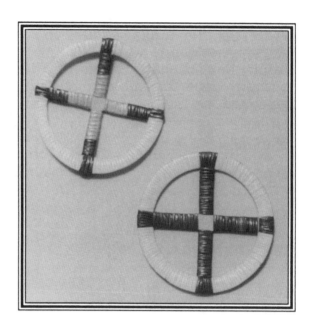

The significance of the *Quilled Medicine Wheel* was such that it was common to many of the Tribes and Nations of the North American continent. Among other meanings, the *Medicine Wheel* represents the Sacred Circle and the Four Directions. They were, and are, commonly found on bags, pouches, articles of clothing, etc. and are found in ceremonials.

Before beginning, read all of the instructions through carefully so that you know how each step fits into making the completed *Quilled Medicine Wheels*. Do not be afraid to change or personalize the *Wheels* after you understand how they are made. Then follow the instructions through step-by-step.

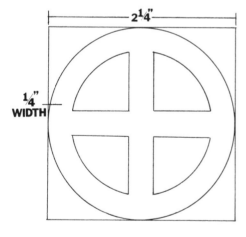

Figure 1

MATERIALS NEEDED

2   Thin rawhide - 2 1/4" x 2 1/4"
1   Thin practice rawhide - 1/4" x 3"
1   Foot imitation sinew
1   Oz. natural porcupine quills
1   Oz. dyed porcupine quills

(1) From thin rawhide, make two pieces that measure 2 1/4" x 2 1/4" square. From these use a craft knife and cut out your *Medicine Circles*, or spoked wheels, making sure that every surface is exactly 1/4" in width as shown in **Figure 1**.

(2) Quills become very soft and pliable when wet and then get hard again when they dry. Traditionally quill workers would soften quills by putting them in their mouths but, as this can be very dangerous, we suggest you do not do this. Instead, place the quills to be used in a bowl of water and keep it close to your work.

(3) From the quills, choose those that are thin and 2 inches or longer. Wash them in hot soapy water until clean of any oils and let dry. Dyed porcupine quills may be purchased from many craft stores or you may choose to dye them yourself with any good organic dye or with natural materials - a little vinegar will help set the color.

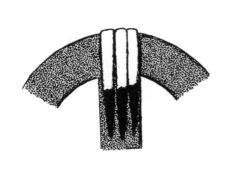

Figure 2

(4) To begin quilling, take one of the wheels made in *Step 1* and add three soft quills that have been flattened as shown in **Figure 2**. These go at the four junctions where the wheel meets the cross bars. Make sure that the ends of the quills completely cover the wheel in both the front and back and that the black area of the quill does not show. The quills may be held in place by either of these two methods:

(4a) Split the imitation sinew provided into very fine threads. Then holding the quills in position, tie the bottoms of the quills securely in place by wrapping one of the threads around the rawhide and make a small knot. Then cut off the excess imitation sinew. Or,

(4b) The easiest and most common manner to hold the quills in place is to use a very small drop of glue on both the front and bottom quill tips. This may not be traditional but is much easier and will hold the quills in place securely. Let any glue used dry before progressing.

(5) After one set (usually three or four) of quills have been secured in place, the wrapping technique (**Figure 3**) begins down one of the spokes: Hold the rounded end (or "bottom") of the quill against the top of the first rawhide 1/4" spoke with your left hand. The quill should be pointing with the black, pointed end up toward the wheel and slightly to the left. Then, holding the bottom in position, wrap the quill to the right (**Figure 3a**), making sure not to twist it, and wrap it completely around the rawhide spoke. Continue around and over the bottom of the quill holding it in place. There may be a small amount of twisting of the rounded tip to accomplish this (**Figure 3b**).

(6) Continue wrapping the quill around the rawhide until you get to the black area at the point, or "top." The black part of the quill should not show on the front of the wheel and when this area is reached, stop wrapping and make a downward twist of the quill tip laying the tip along the center of the strip with the point going down the spoke. To do this (**Figure 3c**) make a "groove" at about a 45° angle on the quill with your thumb and fold it over itself and pointing down.

(7) Using your left hand, hold the wrapped quill in place and, with your right hand, insert the rounded bottom of a new softened quill under the twist of the previous quill (**Figure 3d**). Fold this quill to the left, over the point of the first

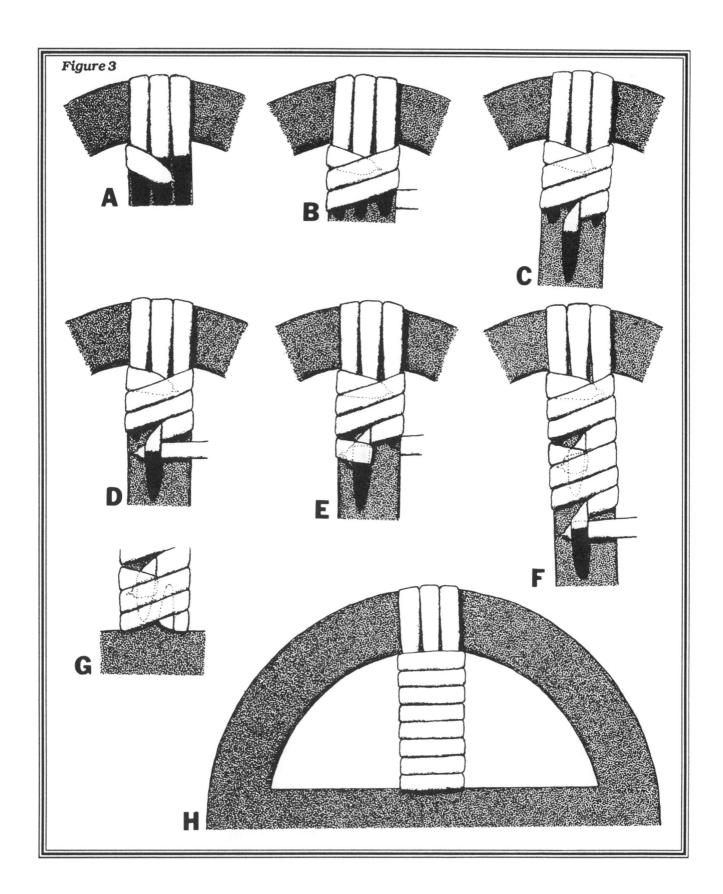

Figure 3

A

B

C

D

E

F

G

H

59

quill (*Figure 3e*), and repeat the wrapping (as above) making sure that the point is held securely under the wrapping. Continue down the rawhide making sure that each successive wrap is as close to the previous wrap as possible to make sure that the rawhide does not show on the front and that both the top and bottom of the last quill are securely covered (wrapped) on the back (*Figure 3f*).

(8) The first couple of quills are sometimes difficult to start but the others will begin to lay in nicely as the work progresses. Continue to wrap the rawhide until the junction of the spokes has been reached (the junction will not be quilled). At this point twist the black tip up under the quill wrapping, pull it snug and let it set to dry (*Figure 3g*). *Figure 3h* shows the front of the quilled spoke.

(9) With the wrapping technique now mastered, the rest of the wheel will be much easier. Now repeat this technique on the remaining three spokes.

(10) Start at the back of the wheel, next to one set of the "glued" quills and use the wrapping technique around the wheel until the next set of quills is reached (*Figure 4*). At this point use the ending described in *Figure 3g*. Then quill the remaining three spaces between the spokes on the wheel.

Figure 4

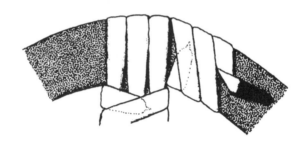

HINTS

(A) While quill work is not the easiest craft to do correctly, it certainly is not as difficult as most people think. Still, for the beginning craftsperson it is a good idea to practice these basics before starting a larger project. The "Materials" list includes a 1/4" piece of rawhide to be used for practice.

(B) It is suggested that you use both natural and dyed quills so that you may incorporate a design of your choosing.

(C) For those who wish for more information on quillwork, the best source of instruction available at this time is *The Techniques of Porcupine Quill Decoration Among the Indians of North America by William C. Orchard.*

(D) All quills should be flattened before use when wrapping. The quills may be flattened by placing them on any flat surface and pulling your thumb nail, while pushing down, across the entire length of the softened quill. Any flat instrument, like the edge of a butter knife, may be used in place of the thumb nail.

DANCE BELL

SET

This *Dance Bell Set* is designed for fancy dancers, grass dancers and hobbyists who enjoy Indian dancing. While the directions show how to use sleigh bells, you could substitute cow bells or brass bells and use essentially the same techniques. In any event, it is important to read the instructions through so that you understand how each step fits into making the completed project and then, as you make your *Dance Bell Set*, feel free to improvise in any way that will make them more suited to your needs. As with any project, take your time to insure that the finished product is done as well as you expect.

MATERIALS NEEDED

1	Piece soft strap leather 2" x 14"
1	Piece imitation angora 2" x 14"
2	Leather boot laces 36" long
10	1 1/2" sleigh bells
2	Feet imitation sinew
1	#8 Glover's or leather needle

(1) The first thing to do is measure the distance around your leg at the place where you will be wearing the *Dance Bell Set.* As you will be using the imitation angora for padding (below), be sure and allow for that extra distance. If the measurement is less than 14" (and it probably will be), you will have to cut some material from the end of the strap leather required in the list above. If you are not sure of the most comfortable length for the strap, leave it a little long and allow for this when you make the holes for mounting the bells; you can always cut off the extra leather after using the bells once or twice as it is hard to add more leather later.

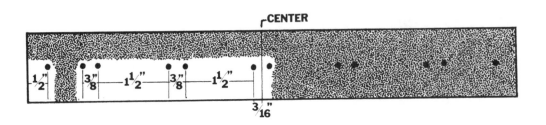

Figure 1

(2) Cut the strap leather into two (2) pieces, each 1" wide x 14" long. (The following measurements are given for a strap 14" long. If your measurement from *Step 1* is longer or shorter you will have to adjust the position of the bells accordingly.) On one piece, mark the exact center with a pencil and then, as shown in **Figure 1**, measure to the right and make marks at 3/16", 1 1/2", 3/8", 1 1/2" and 3/8". Then, 1/2" from the end, make another mark. Then measure to the left and make marks at 3/16", 1 1/2", 3/8", 1 1/2", and 3/8". One-half inch from the end of this side, make another mark.

(3) Do the same thing on the other piece of strap leather.

(4) Use a leather punch, awl or other pointed instrument (Be Careful!) and punch holes at each mark made in the two pieces. We recommend using a leather punch as it will make stringing the thong much easier.

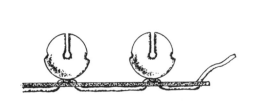

Figure 2

(5) As shown in **Figure 2**, starting in the middle of one of the thongs and from the center of one of the straps, string the thong and the bells to the strap. Be sure and leave plenty of thong extending from each side as these are your tie strings and must go around your leg and be easy to adjust and secure. Now repeat this step for the other strap.

(6) Cut the imitation angora into two pieces that are each 1" x 14" (or the length of your strap leather). These should exactly match the strap leather pieces to which the bells are mounted.

(7)   Split the imitation sinew into three or four pieces. Using one of the "threads" of imitation sinew and the glover's needle, sew the imitation angora to the back of the strap leather as shown in **Figure 3**. Make sure that the "fuzzy" side of the imitation angora is facing out (will be next to your leg) when it is sewn in place.   Be sure to make nice even stitches about 1/8" apart and about 1/8" from the outside of the material. Depending upon the thickness of the strap leather, it may be difficult to push the glover's needle through it and you may find it helpful to make your "sewing holes" with an awl. If you choose to do this, it is suggested that it be done after *Step 4* and before *Step 5*.

Figure 3

NOTES

TRADITIONAL INDIAN

CRAFTS

with

FEATHERS

NOTES

FEATHERED

DANCE WHISTLE

The *Feathered Dance Whistle* has always been used for ceremonial purposes by the Indians of the Plains and was usually made from the wing bone of an eagle. The whistle was used during dances and other religious activities. As it is illegal for non-Indians to possess or use eagle feathers or parts (such as wing bones), we suggest the use of either wood or bamboo whistles.

Remember to read through all of the instructions so that you understand how each step fits into making the finished product before you begin. Then take your time as you construct your *Feathered Dance Whistle*. Don't be afraid to improvise as the "Materials" list should be considered the minimum requirements and by adding bells, beads, claws, teeth, etc. a most attractive finished project is possible.

MATERIALS NEEDED

1 Whistle (wood or bamboo)
8 Fluffs (5-6")
2 Imitation eagle feathers
3 Feet imitation sinew or "F" thread
1 Suede thong (6")
1 Suede thong (10")
1 Oz craft glue - optional

(1) If you want to paint the whistle or decorate it, use some fine sand paper and lightly sand the whistle so that the wood is smooth. Then decorate as desired.

(2) Tie the short thong around the end of the whistle with a square knot so that both ends of the thong hang down about even on both sides.

(3) Use the imitation sinew and tie 2 fluffs to each end of the thong. The "thread" is going to show, so be sure and make an attractive wrap around the thong and make the knots small. If there is not enough quill showing at the bottom of the fluffs, you can cut off a little of the fluff to make it easier to tie.

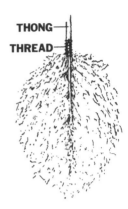

Figure 1

(4) Tie the long thong around the whistle half-way between the whistle mouth piece and the first air hole. Use the square knot and leave one of the ends of the thong hanging about 1" lower than the other end.

(5) Starting with one of the thongs, lay one of the feathers so that the webbing is even with the end of the thong and the quill is pointing toward the whistle. Start at the quill point and, with the thread, tie the feather to the thong by taking the thread around and around both quill and thong. When you have wrapped almost all of the feather's quill to the thong, place a fluff on top of the feather so that the "fluffy" part covers the lower webbing and the fluff's quill points toward the whistle. Then continue wrapping the thread around the thong, feather quill and the quill of the fluffs. Keep in mind that this wrapping will show so make it even and attractive.

You might want to use a very small spot of glue on the fluff quills, but if the wrapping is neat and tight this should not be necessary.

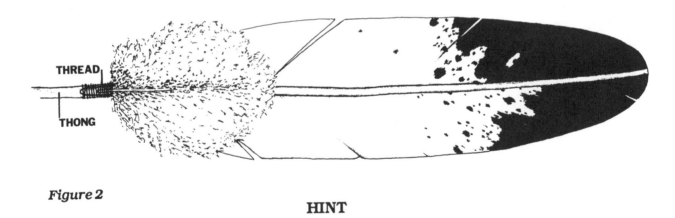

Figure 2

HINT

(A) With the imitation sinew, to make the thread, cut it into two pieces that are 18" long and then split the sinew into four strips or "threads" for use in wrapping.

68

SINGLE or DANCING

FEATHER

The "*Single Feather*" was traditionally carried by dancers and used in sweat lodges and was made from the feather of a sacred bird, usually an eagle. Today it is still seen at pow wows and ceremonials but is also used as a mirror decoration, hat feather, hair tie, scalp lock and for many other uses; in that it is illegal to possess or use eagle feathers, most are made from hand-painted or commercially prepared turkey feathers.

As with all of the projects in this book, it is suggested that before starting you read through the instructions carefully so that you understand how each step fits into making the *Single Feather* and do not be afraid to be creative and change the project to suit your own taste.

MATERIALS NEEDED

1	Imitation Eagle Feather
2	Short white fluffs
2	Long white fluffs
1	3" x 1 1/2" split leather piece
1	#8 Glover's (leather) needle
1	Yard of imitation sinew
8	Pieces of horse hair (any color)
1	3" suede leather thong
1	Yard black lacing thread
1	Oz. craft glue

69

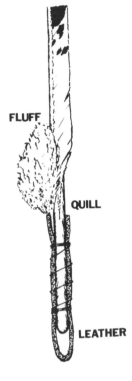

FLUFF

QUILL

LEATHER

Figure 1

(1) If the feather is not as straight as you want, simply hold the spine or quill close to a 100 watt light bulb and as it gets warm, straighten it with your fingers. Another method that works faster, but is a bit harder, is to hold the spine in steam (as from a tea pot) and work the feather into shape. In either case, be careful: The same heat that shapes the feather can burn your fingers.

(2) Split the imitation sinew into three or four "threads" so that it is easy to work with.

(3) Place the feather on a table with the quill end toward you. Place the two long fluffs so that they are on top of the feather with their quill ends on the exposed quill of the feather. Use a "thread" of imitation sinew to tie them in place. You may also use a small drop of glue, but it should not be necessary. If you are not going to hang the feather, go to *Step 5*.

(4) If you are going to hang the feather instead of carrying it, form a loop with the 3" thong and place it at the very end of the feather's quill. With a "thread" of imitation sinew, tie this securely in place (***Figure 1***). You might want to use a spot of craft glue on the ends of the thong, but it should not be necessary if you tie it tightly.

(5) This is the most difficult step in making the project and the one that will add the most to it: With the 3" x 1 1/2" split leather piece (this may be done with felt, if desired), measure it so that it is long enough at the bottom to cover the ends of the loop, leaving the loop part exposed, and at the top to cover the quill part of the fluffs, leaving the fluffy part showing. Cut it into this length. Then wrap the leather (or felt) around the feather and measure it so that it is almost wide enough to wrap around the quill of the feather. Cut this width. Then wrap it around the quill again and make sure that in width the ends almost come together. If it is too long, trim off the excess. Make sure that your first cut is not too short!

(6) Put the feather "face down," or with the fluffs, loop and front of the feather against the table. Put one of the "threads" of imitation sinew on the needle and place the leather or felt around the quill. Then use a cross stitch to sew it in place. The leather has some "give" to it and as you sew, bring the ends of it together so that they meet. ***Figure 2*** shows the ends apart, but that is just to show the stitch.

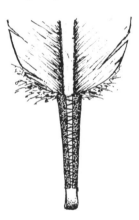

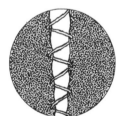

Figure 2

(7) Cut the black lacing thread into two pieces and wrap them around the bottom part of the feather (see **Figure 3**). After knotting, leave the ends hanging down as shown.

(8) Place the feather so that the top is toward you. Clip off any quills that may be on the short fluffs and lay the fluffs close by. Straighten the horsehair, make a bunch of it with all of one of the ends even and put it where you can get it in a hurry. Now, place a small spot of glue on the front quill of the feather about 1/2" from the top. Place the even ends of the horsehair in the glue and then place the small fluffs on top of the glue and horsehair ends so that they extend just a little beyond the feather. Gently press on the spine of the fluffs just over the glue spot but be sure and glue only the spines to the feather and that the fluffs stay "fluffy."

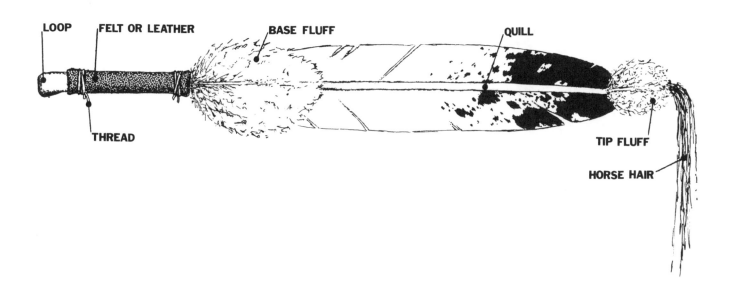

CRAFT TECHNIQUES

SHAPING FEATHERS

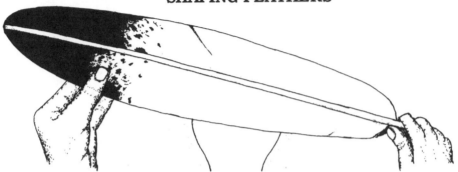

Often when you do craft work with feathers it happens that those that are supplied or purchased need to be improved to match other feathers that will be used in the project. Almost all feathers should be trimmed at the top to make them more attractive but often some will not have enough curve, or have too much, and there are two techniques that may be used to correct this. **(1)** The first procedure is to run the quill of the feather next to a 100 watt light bulb to heat the quill and then to use your thumb and forefinger to mold the curve as you want it. To do this, heat first the front of the quill, mold the curve, then heat the back of the quill and mold further, and so forth. **(2)** Or, you can run the quill of the feather over steam. First the front, then the back and then mold the quill into the shape you desire. In either case, it is a good idea to repeat the procedure about 24 hours after you do it the first time. Also, in both cases, extreme care should be taken to protect your eyes and fingers. Take the feather away from the light and steam before trying to mold the quill to the shape needed.

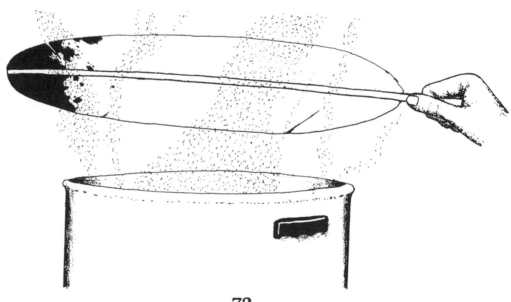

QUILLED

SINGLE or DANCING

FEATHER

The Quilled Single Feather was traditionally carried by dancers and used in sweat lodges and was made from the feather of a sacred bird, usually an eagle. Today it is still used for these purposes as well as for a mirror decoration, hat feather, hair tie, scalp lock, etc. As it is illegal to possess or use real eagle feathers, most are now made from hand-painted or commercially prepared turkey feathers.

Before starting the construction of this project, read through the instructions carefully so that you know how each step fits into making your completed Quilled Single Feather and do not be afraid to personalize or change the project to suit your own needs. Where glue is called for, a fast

MATERIALS NEEDED

1	Imitation Eagle Feather
2	Short white fluffs
2	Long white fluffs
1	3" x 1 1/5" split leather piece
1	#8 Glover's (leather) needle
3	Feet imitation sinew
12	Pieces horse hair (any color)
1	3" suede leather thong
1	Yard black lacing thread
1	1/4" x 12" (approx) rawhide strip
1	1/4 Oz. natural porcupine quills
1	1/2 Oz. dyed porcupine quills
1	Oz. craft glue

drying organic glue will work well and be sure and use only a small amount. If you are opposed to using glue because of authenticity, use imitation sinew split into a number of thin threads and use it to tie the parts together. If you do this, it is important to use a fine thread, to make small knots and to cut off the excess imitation sinew when finished.

Quill Preparation

(1) From the quills, choose those that are 2 inches or longer and thin. Wash them in hot soapy water until clean of any oils. Let dry.

(2) Dyed porcupine quills may be purchased from many craft stores or you may choose to dye them yourself with any good organic dye - a little vinegar will help set the color.

(3) Quills must be softened before using. The traditional method is to place the quills in the mouth as the saliva works to soften them. However, as this can be very dangerous, we cannot recommend it and if you choose this method you should limit the number of quills in your mouth to one or two. Another, safer and suggested method is to keep a small bowl of water with quills in it next to your work.

Preparation of the Quilled Strip

Figure 1

Figure 2

(4) First, you have to make sure the 1/4" rawhide strip is the correct length. Lay the rawhide next to the feather; it should go from the tip of the feather down to about 1/2" below the end of the feather webbing on the quill (**Figure 1**).

(5) As shown in **Figure 2,** use a small amount of glue to secure the horsehair and the two small fluffs to the end (this will be the "top") of the rawhide strip. The fluff part of these feathers should cover the very end of the rawhide strip with the quill part going down the strip and enough of the horse hair (about an inch) should be glued in place to make it secure. The quilling (below) will help keep the fluffs and horse hair in place but you want to make sure that they do not come loose while you work or at a later time. The side these are secured to will be the "front" of the rawhide strip.

(6) All of the quill work technique is done on the back of the rawhide strip, so turn the strip over so that the front faces away from you. The technique for using the quills is shown in **Figures 3a** through **3h.** Using a softened quill (they will become hard again when they dry), make it flat. Now, hold the rounded end (or bottom) of the quill against

74

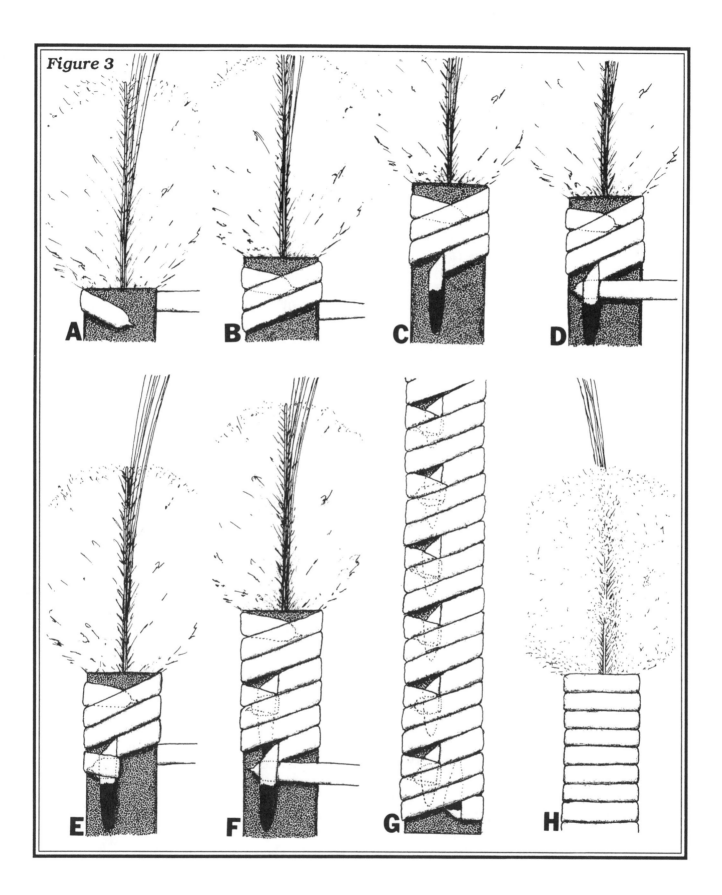

the top of the rawhide strip with your left hand. The quill should be pointing with the black, pointed end up toward the top and slightly to the left. Then, holding the bottom in position, wrap the quill to the right (**Figure 3a**), making sure not to twist it, and wrap it completely around the rawhide strip. Continue around, covering the bottom of the fluff and horse hair in front, and over the bottom of the quill, in back, holding it in place. There may be a small amount of twisting of the rounded tip to accomplish this (**Figure 3b**).

(7) Continue wrapping the quill around the rawhide until you get to the black area at the point, or top. The black part of the quill should not show on the front of the strip so when this area is reached, stop wrapping and make a downward twist of the quill tip laying the tip along the center of the strip with the point going down the strip. To do this (**Figure 3c**), with your thumb nail make a "groove" at about a 45 angle on the quill and fold it over itself and pointing down.

(8) Using your left hand, hold the wrapped quill in place and, with your right hand, insert the rounded bottom of a new softened quill under the twist of the previous quill (**Figure 3d**). Fold this quill to the left, over the point of the first quill (**Figure 3e**) and repeat the wrapping (*above*) making sure that the point is held securely under the wrapping. Continue down the rawhide making sure that each successive wrap is as close to the previous wrap as possible to make sure that the rawhide does not show on the front and that both the top and bottom of the last quill are securely covered (wrapped) on the back (**Figure 3f**).

(9) The first couple of quills are sometimes difficult to start but the others will begin to lay in nicely as the work progresses. Continue to wrap the rawhide until you reach about 1/4" from the bottom of the rawhide strip. At this point twist the black tip of the last quill up under the quill wrapping, pull it snug and let it set to dry (**Figure 3g**). **Figure 3h** shows the front of the top part of the quilled rawhide.

Preparation of the Feather

(10) If the feather you have is not as straight as you want, simply hold the spine or quill close to a 100 watt light bulb and as it gets warm, straighten it with your fingers. You may also use steam. In any event be careful, as the same heat that straightens the feather will burn fingers.

(11) Split the imitation sinew into three or four "threads" so that it is easy to work with.

(12) Place the feather on a table, face up, and lay the quilled strip on top of it so that the strip covers the feather's quill and the top is even with the top of the feather (**Figure 4**). When it is in the right position, use a small amount of glue on the feather quill and secure the strip in place. Allow to dry completely.

(13) With the feather face up and the quill end toward you, place the two long fluffs so that they are on top of the quilled strip and the bottom of the feather webbing is even with the fluff feathers. Use a thread of imitation sinew to tie

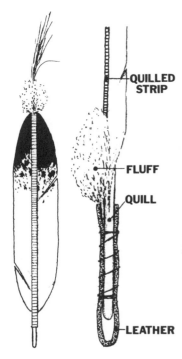

Figure 4   *Figure 5*

QUILLED STRIP

FLUFF

QUILL

LEATHER

these in place. You may also use a small drop of glue, but it should not be necessary.

(**14**) Form a loop with the 3" thong and place it at the very end of the feather's quill (*Figure 5*). With a thread of imitation sinew, tie this securely in place. Again, a small drop of glue may be used here but should not be necessary if it has been tied in tightly.

(**15**) Take your time with this next step as it is fairly difficult but adds much to the look of the finished feather if done right: Measure the split leather piece so that it is long enough at the bottom to cover the ends of the loop, leaving the loop part outside, and, at the top, to cover the bottom of the quilled strip and the quill part of the fluffs, leaving the "fluffy" (webbing) part exposed. Cut it into this length. Then wrap the leather around the feather and measure it so that it is almost wide enough to wrap around the quill of the feather. Cut it this width. Now wrap it around the quill again and make sure that in width the ends almost come together. If it is too long, trim off the excess. Make sure that your first cut is not too short!

(**16**) Put the feather "face down" or with the quilled strip, fluffs and front of the feather against the table. Put one of the threads of imitation sinew on the needle and place the leather around the quill. Then use a cross stitch (*Figure 6*) to sew it in place. The leather has some "give" to it and as you sew, bring the ends of it together so that they meet. *Figure 6* shows the ends apart, but that is just to show the stitch.

(**17**) Cut the black lacing thread into two pieces and wrap them around the leather piece near the bottom and near the top (*Figure 7*). After knotting, leave the ends hanging down as shown.

HINTS

(**A**) While quill work is not the easiest craft to do correctly, it certainly is not as difficult as most people think and good quill workers maintain that it is as easy and fast as beadwork after the basics are mastered. Still, for the beginning craftsperson it is a good idea to practice the basic technique (**Figure 3**) on a 1/4" rawhide strip before starting the project.

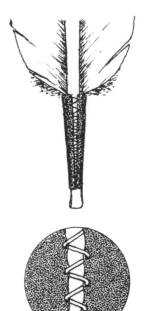

Figure 6

(B) The "Material" list suggests both natural and dyed quills so that you may make a design in the quilled strip. Simply plan your work so that the dyed quills are used at the proper time.

(C) The best source of information available at this time is **The Techniques of Porcupine Quill Decoration Among the Indians of North America** by Wm. C. Orchard. A copy of that book will reveal the following information that may be helpful with any quill project: (1) Tools: On pages 14-15, Orchard describes and explains the various tools that may be used in quill work. (2) Dyeing: Various sources of dyes are described on pages 9-14. (3) Techniques to do quill work are explored throughout the book, but the technique used in this project is described and illustrated on page 19.

(D) All quills should be flattened before use when wrapping. Traditional quill workers would soften the quills by holding them in their mouths and then would flatten them by pulling them out of their mouth between the upper and lower teeth. As noted, this can be dangerous. The quills may be flattened by placing them on any flat surface and pulling your thumb nail, while pushing down, across the entire length of the softened quill. Any flat instrument, like the edge of a butter knife, may be used in place of the thumb nail.

(E) The very best "hint" that can be given regarding quill work, like beadwork, is to take your time and do not rush the project. The best looking finished products, for example, usually take the most time and planning.

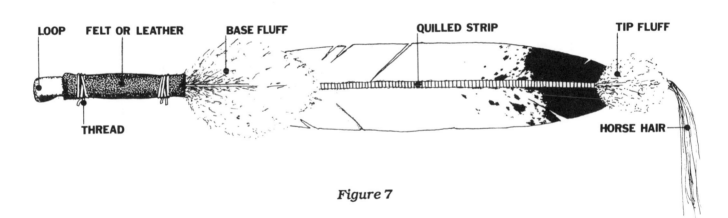

Figure 7

FANCY DANCE BUSTLE

In the culture of the American Indian the dance is an intricate part of ceremonials and religion and the dance bustle, in one form or another, has existed since pre-history. With the introduction of modern dyes, the natural feathers that were used to make bustles took on bright hues and the *Fancy Dance Bustle* became, in action, a riot of color. Today this fantastic Bustle may be seen at pow wows throughout the country with contestants competing for thousands of dollars. This project is fairly difficult and will produce a professional *Fancy Dance Bustle*.

Before beginning, read through all of the instructions carefully so that you know how each step fits into the total project. Then follow the instructions step-by-step and take your time! This is a very beautiful *Bustle* if it is made with a lot of time and patience.

MATERIALS NEEDED

72	12-14" turkey wing spikes*
144	2-3" fluffs
4	Oz 5-6" fluffs
7	Oz 6-8" dark hackles
2	Oz horse hair
14	Feet imitation sinew
3	Bobbins "D" thread
4	60" Leather boot laces
1	6" x 55" red felt
1	3" beaded rosette
1	4" beaded rosette
2	6" x 5" plywood boards
1	Piece poster board 14" x 14"
2	Wire coat hangers
1	Oz craft glue
1	Roll adhesive or plastic tape

(*) You will need 36 "lefts" and 36 "rights." See Step #1.

Preparing the Feathers

(1) Lay all of the feathers face-up (with the exposed quill down) in front of you. Some of the feathers will naturally curve to the right (called "rights") and some to the left (called "lefts"). Place the rights on your right side and the lefts to the left and keep these two groups separate throughout the rest of the project.

(2) If any of the feathers curve too much or not enough, they may be shaped. Simply run the quill next to a light bulb (be careful of the heat and protect your eyes). Apply a gentle, steady pressure on the quill until it takes the correct shape. It may help to turn the feather over so that you heat both sides evenly. If there is any misplaced webbing, heat it over a steaming teapot and then preen the webbing into place with your fingers. When all of the feathers look just as you want them, go to the next step.

(**3**) Now you want to make all of the feathers, lefts and rights, the same length: As shown in **Figure 1**, you want to trim off the top and quill ends to do this. Then, trim the webbing as shown at both top and bottom.

(**4**) As illustrated in **Figure 2** (side view), trim about 1/4" of the quill end so that the bottom comes to a sharp point. This point is then folded up into the quill itself to form a 1/8" loop (the leather thong will go through these loops). Put a drop of glue inside the quill to hold the loop securely in place.

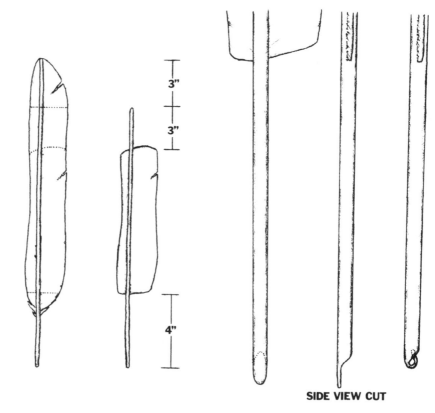

SIDE VIEW CUT

Figure 1   *Figure 2*

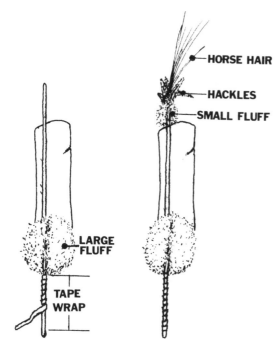

HORSE HAIR

HACKLES

SMALL FLUFF

LARGE FLUFF

TAPE WRAP

Figure 3   *Figure 4*

(**5**) Cut off about 12" of imitation sinew and split it into three or four "threads." Using these threads, tie the base (5-6") fluffs in place (**Figure 3**) putting two in front and two in back of the feather. Then wrap the base with adhesive or colored plastic tape and overlap the fluff quill ends where they were tied.

(**6**) Divide the horsehair, hackles and fluffs into 72 small bunches. Approximately 2" down from the tip of each spike, tie a bunch of horsehair into place and, without knotting the "thread," tie in the hackles and then make a good secure knot. Then, just above the webbing, tie in the fluffs - they should hide the thread around the horsehair and hackles and come to the bottom of the hackles (**Figure 4**). A small amount of glue may be used during this step but keep the fluffy part of the hackles and fluffs free. Now separate the feathers into two groups: 1/2 of the lefts and 1/2 of the rights in each set.

Making the Bustle

(**7**) String a thong through the quill loops of each set of your feathers and tie tightly to make a complete circle - do not cut off the excess thong as you will want to adjust the circle when you mount the sets to the boards (below). Make sure that all of the rights are on the right side and all of the lefts are on the left. Then make a light mark on the back of each feather that is 5" above the loop. With a small sharp awl, or needle, make a hole through the quill at this point. Thread the imitation sinew (full strength) through the hole in the upper left-hand spike leaving about 6" of the sinew exposed (this will be used to tie to the wires on the base). Then proceed through the hole of the next left and continue down through all of the lefts, then the rights, until you reach the top-most right. Leave a 6" tie and cut off the extra imitation sinew (**Figure 5**).

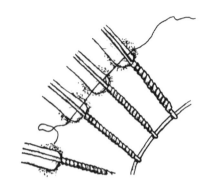

Figure 5

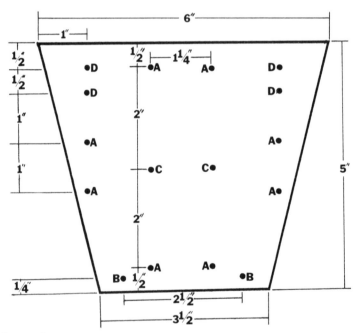

Figure 6

(**8**) Cut and drill two bustle frames from plywood following the pattern in **Figure 6**. All holes, except those marked "D", should be about 1/4" in diameter; holes "D" should be about the same size as a coat hanger.

(**9**) Bend pieces of coat hanger through holes "D" as shown in **Figure 7** to which the feathers will be tied. Lay the tied feathers (*Step 7*) on the base so that the tied circle touches all of the holes labled "A" and from the underside of the base, use a long thong to lace the circle to the frame (**Figure 8**).

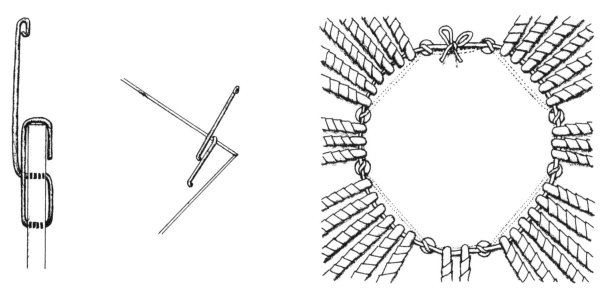

Figure 7   **Figure 8**

(10) Cut two circles of stiff poster board; one has a diameter of 5" and the other 7". Out of each, cut a triangle shaped piece that has a base of 1". On each circle you want to lace it back together so that it forms a slight cone (**Figure 9**). Put a liberal amount of glue on the inside of the cone and carefully place fluffs and hackles around the cone.

(11) With the feathers attached to the base, space the feathers evenly and then, with imitation sinew, attach the cones by lacing a rosette through each cone and to the base through the holes marked "C" (**Figure 10**).

(12) In the top (neck) base, tie a pair of thongs through holes "B" that will tie around your chest. In the back base, holes "B" may be used for thongs to go around your waist. Additional neck and waist thongs may be added as needed.

(**Figure 9** and **Figure 10** on next page)

83

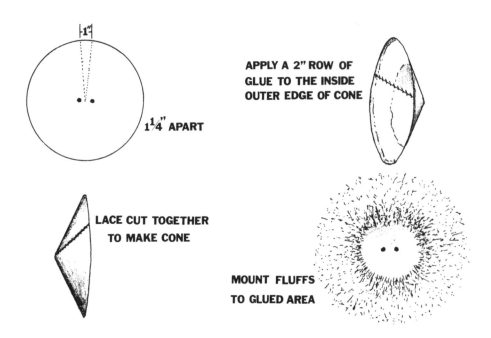

|-1"-|

$1\frac{1}{4}$" APART

LACE CUT TOGETHER
TO MAKE CONE

APPLY A 2" ROW OF
GLUE TO THE INSIDE
OUTER EDGE OF CONE

MOUNT FLUFFS
TO GLUED AREA

Figure 9

Figure 10

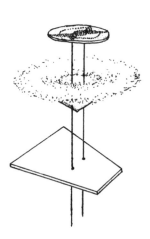

84

DOUBLE

TRAILER

WARBONNET

The *Double Trailer Warbonnet* is the headdress that is most commonly associated with the Indian chief and is one of the most beautiful items of traditional Indian dress. This item was only used for "best dress" and may be seen today at pow wows and ceremonials on the upper and lower Plains and at museums throughout the world.

This project is fairly difficult and will require a considerable investment in labor and materials. Before beginning, be sure and read the instructions carefully so that you can visualize how each step fits into the finished *Warbonnet* and then, as you follow the instructions step-by-step to construct the project, take your time.

MATERIALS NEEDED

90	12-14" imitation eagle feathers*
180	2-3" fluffs
180	5-6" fluffs
1	27" x 4 1/2" scrap leather
1	5" x 72" red felt
1	7" x 72" red felt
1	1 1/2 Oz of horse hair
3	Leather boot laces 72" long
2	Bobbins "D" nymo thread
10	Yards imitation sinew
1	Small rabbit skin
2	Beaded rosettes - 1 1/2" diameter
1	Beaded strip - 12" long
1	Turkey spike
1	11" x 15" split leather piece
1	Oz craft glue

(*) - The feathers should be half "rights" and half "lefts". See *Step 5* for instructions.

Construction of the Crown

(**1a**) The crown may be made out of felt or leather and if you can find an old leather or felt hat with a round crown, a good felt cap or a leather "skull cap" that fits your head snuggly, simply make the crown adjustable as shown in **Figure 1**: Cut a triangle out of the crown that is about 3" high and has a base 1" long. Punch three holes on each side of the triangle, thread a shoe lace through the holes and use this for adjustments.

OR

Figure 1

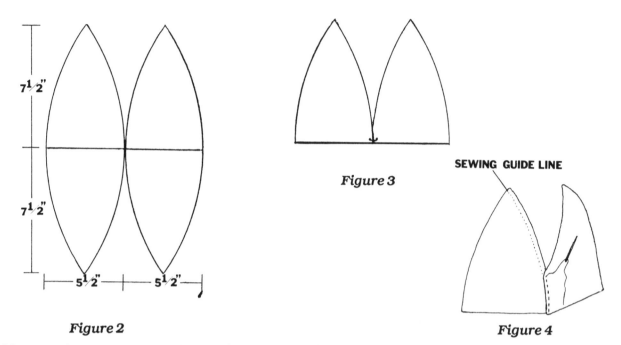

Figure 2

Figure 3

SEWING GUIDE LINE

Figure 4

(1b) As this step provides a foundation for the whole project it may be preferable to construct a sturdy leather crown. If you choose this option, take your time and work carefully. From the 11" x 15" piece of suede or split leather, cut four pieces as shown in **Figure 2**. These will form the leather crown. Note: If your head is smaller than 10 1/2" around, use the measurements used in these directions; if it is larger, you will have to make the crown proportionally larger.

(2) To insure that the crown fits properly, "tack" the bottom together by making a single secure loop of imitation sinew in the bottom corner of each piece as shown in **Figure 3**. Then place the "crown" on your head. It should fit snuggly. If the crown is not snug enough (and it probably will not be) you will have to estimate how much tighter it has to be. Remove one "tack," overlap the leather 1/4 of the distance you need to shorten and retack the pieces together with a single secure loop of imitation sinew. Do this at each tack. Then try the crown on your head again. If it still is not just right, re-do this procedure. This step may take more time than you would like but it is very important that the crown fits correctly so it is worth the extra time and effort.

(3) When the crown fits just right, make a mark with a pencil where the leather overlaps at each corner you have tacked. Then remove the tacks. If the mark you made is, for example, 1/8" from the edge of the leather, continue a line up the side of the piece that is 1/8" from the edge. This will be your sewing guide so make sure that the distance is correct and the same on each piece.

(4) Now using a running stitch (**Figure 4**), keep the overlap on your sewing guide and sew the pieces into place forming the finished crown. If all has gone well, it will fit just as it should - snug, but not too tight.

Preparing the Feathers

(5) Lay all of the feathers face-up (with the exposed quill down) in front of you. Those feathers that naturally curve to the right are called "rights" and those that curve to the left are "lefts." You will need 45 lefts and 45 rights.

(6) If any of the feathers curve too much or not enough, they may be shaped by simply running the quill next to a 100 watt light bulb (be careful of the heat and protect your eyes) as shown in **Figure 5.**
Apply a gentle steady pressure on the quill until it takes the correct shape. Do not use too much force or bend the feather or it will make a permanent "crimp." It may help to turn the feather over so that you heat both sides evenly. When all of the feathers look just as you want them, go to the next step.

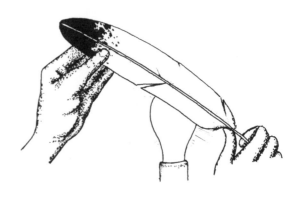

(7) Most natural turkey feathers are rather pointed and you may want to use some sharp scissors and round off the black ends of the feathers. If you choose to do this, be sure that you do not shorten the feathers and make sure that all are shaped the same way.

Figure 5

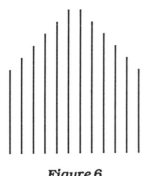

Figure 6

(8) Place all of the feathers in front of you, face up, with the lefts on your left and the rights on your right. Now lay them side by side and arrange the feathers so that the longest left is center-left and the shortest left is farthest to the left; that longest right is center-right and the shortest right is to your extreme right. To do this, place the extreme tip of the quills on a straight line or at the edge of the table. **Figure 6** is a graphic of what you want to achieve with the feathers.

(9) There should be an even and gradual difference between the longest and the shortest feather and both sides should have the same "slope" to it. You can arrange this by shortening or lengthening the feathers:

(10) Decide which side has the best gradual slope to it. Shorten any feather that needs it on that side by cutting off the quill at the base - never cut the black feathered top! Then shape the other side by making sure the matching feather is the same size (in other words, the second feather from the middle-left matches the second feather from the middle-right, and the last feather on the right side matches the last feather on the left side, etc.). Do this by cutting off the quill end. Keep in mind that you need a minimum of 2 1/2" of quill showing below the feather webbing. NOTE: It is very rare to have a bonnet that is perfect in slope on both sides. Also, by adjusting the length of the leather loop and the position of the end fluffs (explained below) a feather can be made to look slightly shorter or longer than it actually is. Keep this in mind as you progress with making the project.

Figure 7

(11) It is not usually necessary, but in some cases the length of a feather may be extended. As shown in **Figure 7**, cut off the end of the quill and glue a small wood dowel into the quill hole. Four tooth picks that have been tied together and glued will also work.

Through the rest of the instructions, keep the feathers in order as you have shaped and placed them.

(12) From the scrap leather, cut a strip 1/4" wide by 4 1/4" in length for each feather. Cut a 12" length of imitation sinew and split it into four threads. As shown in **Figure 8,** place the leather strip around the base of the feather so that it forms a loop, just large enough to put a leather thong through, and use a "thread" of imitation sinew to tie it securely in place. Before knotting the imitation sinew, tie two base (5-6") fluffs into place on the feather. Continue this step until all of the feathers have been done. You may also want to use a small amount of glue on the leather strip and the quill ends of the fluff, but this should not be necessary if the sinew is tight and properly knotted.

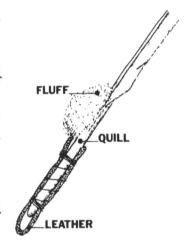

Figure 8

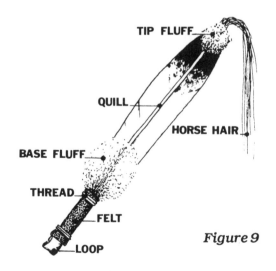

Figure 9

(13) From the felt, cut one piece 1 1/2" wide x 2 1/2" long for each feather. Wrap a piece of the felt around each of the feathers so that it is 2 1/2" long on the quill and the ends meet at the back keeping the leather loop and the body of the fluff outside of the felt. With the white thread, tie the felt around the quill about 1/2" from the bottom and again 1/2" from the top. If horse hair is to be used, glue a small bunch to the very tip of the feather and cover the glue spot with a small fluff (**Figure 9**). You may want to cut the quill ends off of these fluffs before putting it in place. Repeat this step on each of the feathers.

89

Finishing the Crown

(13) Place the bonnet on your head and insure that it fits properly. If you have not made the leather bonnet adjustable, as described above, it may be a good idea, although this can be done after use if it proves necessary.

(14) Sew the beaded strip (browband) into place; if you have made the crown adjustable, the adjustment will be in the back and the browband in the front. Then sew the beaded rosettes in place. If you are putting on rabbit strips or ermine skins, sew them into place just behind the ends of the browband, and sew the rosettes over the top of the skins. If you choose to use leather rosettes they should be painted, quilled and/or beaded before sewing them in place.

(15) Now the "tricky" part: Measure the distance around the crown making allowances for the rosette and browband (**Figure 10**) and call this figure "Y". Divide the measurement ("Y") by 30 (feathers) to get the figure "X". Find the center of the browband and exactly one-half of "X" to the right of center, make your first light mark on the crown just above the browband. Now work your way around the crown to the right making a light mark with each on the distance of "X" away from the last one. You should end up with 30 marks and the last one should be one-half of "X" to the left of center. If you have made the crown adjustable, do not include the 1" space that was cut out in measurement "Y". You will have 15 marks left of center and 15 marks right of center when finished.

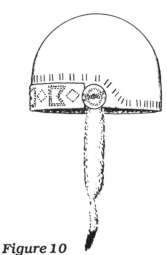

Figure 10

(16) With a sharp knife make a slit 1/4" long that is 1/8" to the side of each mark. This gives you 30 pairs of slits that are 1/4" apart.

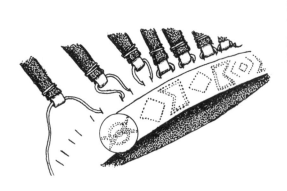

Figure 11

(17) You are going to use only the longest 30 feathers for the crown: Using the leather thong (boot lace), begin at the back center-right of the crown and begin to lace your feathers into position starting with the shortest "right" feather (this is feather #15 on the right) and going around to the longest "right" in the front. Then continue with the longest "left" and keep stringing until you finish with the shortest "left" (feather #15 on the left). (**Figure 11**.) Your lacing should be snug but not tight enough to "pucker" the crown. When everything is in position, tie off the lacing inside the crown.

(18) On the back of each feather make a light mark exactly 6" above the looped end of the quill. Using a small sharp awl or glover's needle, make a hole through each quill where you have marked them.

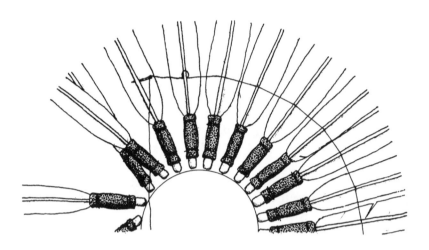

Figure 12

Figure 13

(19) Start at the shortest "left" (rear left-center) and thread imitation sinew through the hole just made. Take all but about 5" of the sinew through the hole. Then thread the lace back through the same hole, making a loop around the quill, and pull fairly tight. Now thread the lace through the hole in the next feather to the left and with 2 1/2" of lace between the feathers, go back through the same hole making a loop around the quill and holding the feathers 2 1/2" apart (**Figure 12**). Continue around the crown to the left until all feathers have been "sewn" into place, leave about 5" of the lacing hanging down after you finish the last feather and cut off the excess. This lacing (imitation sinew) should hold the feathers in place so that the wind will not let it collapse. Tie the sinew at the back and shake the bonnet. If it does not stay as you want it, shorten the space between the feathers until it does.

(20) Using the techniques described above, decorate the turkey spike or plume as you desire but remember that this major plume was always a bit different than the other feathers (**Figure 13**). After you have this plume as you want it, cut two slits in the front-center top of the bonnet and lace it into place as you did with the other feathers.

The Trailer

(21) The difficult part of this project is completed and this part will use the same techniques explained above: Put the bonnet crown on your head and hold the trailer material even with the bottom of the crown at the back. Stand straight and have someone mark the material at a point from the floor where you want the trailer to end. This is a point of personal preference but traditionally it would be no shorter than just below your knees and no longer than 4" above the ground. If you are going to dance, try some movements and make sure that the trailer will never touch the ground. In any event, make sure that, when the trailer is complete, the feathers will never touch the ground. When you have decided the proper length, make an even cut with sharp scissors. NOTE: A double thickness of material will make the trailer hang better. If you decide to sew two pieces together, do it at this point.

(22) Lay the material on a flat surface and place the shortest "right" face-up at the bottom of the material on the right side so that the tip of the feather is about 1/4" from the end. Make a light mark on the material about 1/2" from the edge at the loop of this feather. Now measure 1/2" from the top of the material and make a light mark about 1/2" from the right edge.

(23) Back to the "tricky" parts: Measure the distance between the two marks made on the trailer material and call this figure "Y". Divide this figure ("Y") by 30 (feathers) to get the figure "X". Starting at the mark at the bottom of the material, make a light mark the distance of "X" going up the material and continue until you have 30 marks each the distance of "X" away from each other.

(24) With sharp scissors, make a slit 1/4" long, 1/4" to each side of the light marks so that you have 30 pairs of slits. Fold the material so that the two sides meet, make some light marks through the slits and prepare the left side exactly like the right side. *NOTE:* If you decide to personalize the kit by placing feathers along the bottom or at points in the center of the trailer, be sure and divide "Y" by the actual number of feathers that will go down each side.

The trailer may be attached to the crown either at this time or after the feathers have been attached but we suggest that it be done at this stage so that the lacing can be "anchored" to the bottom of the bonnet.

(25) Using a simple "whip stitch" sew the trailer to the crown (***Figure 14***). If you cut off a short piece of imitation sinew and split it into three or four "threads" it will work just fine. Be sure the trailer is placed at the exact back of the bonnet (opposite the center of the browband) and if you have made the crown adjustable, sew it in place with the adjustment open.

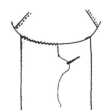

Figure 14

Figure 15

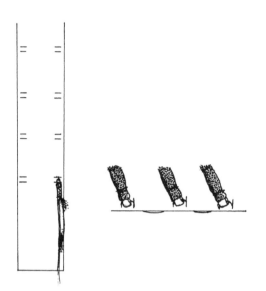

(26)   Starting at the bottom of the trailer, thread the feathers into place using the technique described above on the bonnet. Going up, lace the feathers into place and after the last feather continue the thong up and sew it into the bottom of the crown for additional strength. Be sure that any and all knots are made hidden behind the trailer. (*Figure 15*)

HINTS

(A) Before you begin, count the number of feathers in the project and divide the horsehair, short fluffs and long fluffs into that many groups. Use extra materials on the front crown feathers. Also, if at times you want to use the bonnet without the trailer, lace it into place instead of sewing or you might even want to use Velcro© to hold the trailer.

(B) It is a good idea to look at some good books with pictures of authentic Indian artifacts and to visit museums that feature Indian arts and crafts for additional ideas on how to decorate your Warbonnet, and to read some good books on the Indian culture to understand how and why they were used.

93

NOTES

CRAFT TECHNIQUES

A "Finished" Product

Making your project look "finished" is a combination of techniques but, in general, comes from pre-planning the work and taking your time during construction. Such things as letting glue dry completely before going to the next step will show when the item is ready for examination by your public.

No matter the craft medium, be it bone, leather or feathers, little things like insuring that each knot that is made is as small and neat as possible is as important as making them tight and secure. When you are sewing leather, even if the stitches are hidden on the inside, they should be done as evenly spaced as possible. If you do not take your time with steps like these it will be more than evident on the finished craft.

"Finished" Stitches

Feather Trimming

Taking your time as you prepare the materials to be used is also very important and very few instructions include everything that should be done to make the project more attractive. This means that you have to think through how important each kind of material is to your finished product and what may be done to make it look as good as possible. If you are to use 180 fluffs and you have thirty feathers in the project, you should insure that there are six fluffs on each feather. Before using the fluffs, however, spend the time to trim the feathers so they are all uniform and even.

In all crafts you have to consider the effect that you want to give when someone sees your finished work. An item that is suppose to look just like one made 150 years ago will not be as "polished" as one that is suppose to reflect contemporary crafts and techniques. Still, you want to give the feeling that you have produced the very best article you are capable of making because your craft work is a reflection of yourself. For example, a great deal of leather craft uses either latigo or split leather spacers and the appearance of your end product can be improved greatly with as simple an extra step as taking the time to trim the leather to the shape of the beads or hairpipe.

Finished Leather Spacer

TIC-1/00